EQUINOX

DEVIL'S PARTY PRESS

ISBN: 978-0-9996558-1-8

ACKNOWLEDGMENTS

THE ADMIRAL AND THE WHITE MULBERRY. Copyright © 2018 Mark Alan Polo.
BLACK LACE, BROKEN FEATHERS. Copyright © 2018 William F. Crandell.
CODE RED. Copyright © 2018 Bayne Northern.
DELIA AND CONNECTICUT. Copyright © 2018 Judith Speizer Crandell.
FOR THE COMMON GOOD. Copyright © 2018 David W. Dutton.
THE GIRL IN THE TAFFETA DRESS: A LOVE STORY. Copyright © 2018
David W. Dutton.
HALCYON'S DAYS. Copyright © 2018 David Yurkovich.
PYSANKY SPRING. Copyright © 2018 TJ Lewes.
TRAIN WINDOWS; BALANCED MEALS; WRITING. Copyright © 2018 DD Beals.
WHAT'S THE WORD? BIRD IS THE WORD. Copyright © 2018 Carrie Sz Keane.
WIDDENDREAM. Copyright © 2018 Dianne Pearce.

AWARD-WINNING ANTHOLOGIES FROM DEVIL'S PARTY PRESS

SOLSTICE
(ISBN 9780972264693)

HALLOWEEN PARTY 2017
(ISBN 9780972264686)

CONTENTS

Spring has returned.
The Earth is like a child that knows poems.

Rainer Maria Rilke

The ghostly winter silence had given way to the great spring murmur
of awakening life. This murmur arose from all the land,
fraught with the joy of living.

Jack London

EQUINOX

PREFACE

THE VERNAL EQUINOX IS THE HERALD of spring in the Northern Hemisphere. It is a time of global balance, with winter ending in the north and autumn beginning in the south.

The ten stories and four poems in this anthology focus loosely on that theme—new beginnings, second chances, new relationships, endings, and, of course, espionage.

We open with author David W. Dutton, who offers you a love story that can perhaps best be described as *Springtime in New York* meets *The Sopranos* in "The Girl in the Taffeta Dress: A Love Story."

So much depends upon color in "Widdendream" and "What I Learned From William Carlos Williams," my own humble contributions to this collection that harken back to springs gone by.

In William Crandell's bittersweet tale "Black Lace, Broken Feathers" you learn the fate of Buddy Green, a young, hungry author who values fortune above all else.

Come with me to the past, to a small New Jersey town in 1959, to Mark Polo's "The Admiral and the White Mulberry," a coming-of-age tale played out under the protection of an arbor of blossoms in the heart of the city.

Carrie Sz Keane's haunting essay, "What's the Word? Bird is the Word," begins with the death of a bird. When the small corpse mysteriously disappears you are left contemplating the interconnectedness of nature and humans, from bird feeders to the spinning blades of lawnmowers.

DD Beals presents three short poems ranging in topic from humanity as viewed from a commuter train window to the art of balance to meditative thoughts on the practice of writing.

In "Delia and Connecticut," Judith Speizer Crandell offers up a captivating story in which she brings together two disparate women, each attempting to heal their individual wounds.

"Code Red," a story set against the backdrop of a dying planet, introduces us to GunMic–the one man who, if the stars are aligned, can prevent global extinction, in Bayne Northern's thrilling science fiction tale. Will the world survive?

Picture a cold Vermont landscape, a harsh spring, a man who has lost his way in life. When things seem their most bleak, there is a hand, reaching out. But will it be enough? Author TJ Lewes knows the answer. Find out for yourself in "Pysanky Spring."

David W. Dutton's second entry in this collection, "For the Common Good," introduces us to young Kevin Hopkins. On break from college and visiting family, Kevin finds himself in a dystopian future where he must face a moral crisis greater than any he's ever imagined.

Lastly, travel to London with author David Yurkovich's left-of-center tale of espionage that posits the question: What happens to the office staff when the most secret spy agency in the United Kingdom is suddenly shut down? The grim answer awaits in "Halcyon's Days."

Spring. One day it's warm–a false summer. The next day the wind tests even the strongest roof tiles as rain pelts the cherry blossoms down, down to the earth. Where will Equinox take you–to the flowers, to the Big Apple, or to the stars?

DIANNE PEARCE
Publisher

THE GIRL IN THE TAFFETA DRESS
A Love Story

AUTHOR'S NOTE

Coming up with the idea for a story is not always easy, but sometimes it simply pops into my head. Usually, when this occurs, the premise is rooted in one of my personal memories. At seventy years of age, I have plenty of those.

While composing the two pieces for the anthology, *Solstice,* I suddenly began thinking about an incident that happened back in 1964. I had to fight the urge to put something on paper immediately, but I knew I didn't have the time. The deadline for *Solstice* submittals was rapidly approaching. In spite of that fact, I couldn't shake the girl at the top of the Empire State Building from my mind. She kept popping up, begging to be remembered. That I still could see her vividly should tell you the impression she made upon me on that April afternoon.

As you are about to discover, her time has come, and I feel she would be happy with the finished work. I hope you are, too.

DWD

THE GIRL IN THE TAFFETA DRESS
A Love Story

David W. Dutton

AS STRANGE AS IT MAY seem, Manhattan is much like any other town in America. If you live there and keep a regular schedule, you will encounter the same people day after day after day. This phenomenon will occur on a busy street, on the subway, or in your favorite restaurant. Of course, such encounters do not constitute friendship or even a nodding acquaintance. Certainly not! How would you feel if the other party simply turned their head and walked away? You can't risk that affront to your ego. Still, they are there, populating your little world . . . much like the wallpaper in a long-familiar room. Certainly, there can be exceptions . . . and this may very likely be one of them.

Spring 1964

I love Manhattan in the spring. There is a fresh newness about it. The piles of dirty snow have disappeared. The air is somehow fresher. The acrid smell of exhausts seems to have dissipated or at least sought a higher altitude. The sky is truly blue rather than gray, and the buds in Central Park have begun to sprout. Spring in the city? Sure. Why not?

Although we lived in Greenwich, my parents and I were staying in the city for a couple of nights. I had to complete my registration at Columbia where I would be studying journalism in the fall. Registration was scheduled for Friday, and my mother saw no reason why we shouldn't make a weekend of it. It had been months since we had done anything as a family.

We registered at the Abbey on 7th Avenue at 51st Street. I went my way, and my parents went theirs. We met for dinner at Davy Jones' Locker around the corner from the hotel, also on 51st Street. The shrimp scampi was as delicious as ever . . . one of my father's favorite dishes.

My mother had garnered tickets for a new musical comedy, *High Spirits*, with Tammy Grimes and Beatrice Lillie. It was delightful.

Saturday was clear and moderately warm. The sky was blue and the clouds puffy and white. After a stroll through the Metropolitan, we found ourselves at loose ends.

Lunch was behind us, and it was too early for dinner. On a whim, my father decided on the Empire State Building, noting that on a day like this, the views would be too good to pass up.

The crowd on the observation deck was surprisingly light for such a day, but no one was complaining. My parents and I drifted apart, and I stood watching the people around me. In fact, I was a bit bored. We had been there many times before, but my father was right: The views were clear and crisp. The sun felt good on my face. I leaned against the parapet and folded my arms in front of me.

She darted suddenly from behind the central observation lounge and ran toward one of the many stereo viewers lining the parapet. As she bent to align her eyes with the lenses of the viewer, the sun caught her long, auburn hair and glinted brightly for a brief moment, almost as if there was gold intertwined with the auburn strands.

I was instantly fascinated.

She appeared to be about my age and slim but shapely. The latter was accentuated by the dress she wore. It was unlike what one most saw in the mid-sixties . . . really almost a throwback to the early fifties, but it was obviously expensive. The taffeta fabric was subtly patterned in shades of green. The neckline was a deep scoop, and the sleeves three-quarter in length. The bodice was fitted to the waist where the full skirt fell to just below her knees. A strange choice for an afternoon outing.

Suddenly, she turned from the viewer and ran back the way she had come. I thought to follow her, but she reappeared on the other side of the observation deck before I could do so. There, she ran from viewer to viewer, pausing only seconds at each one. She was like a fairy, a sprite—full of life and sparkle.

As I decided I needed a closer look, she turned and ran toward me. She was laughing . . . at what, I hadn't a clue. Our eyes met briefly in her passing. Mine, brown. Hers, green. Then she was gone, enchanted with the viewer immediately to my left. I turned slowly to look at her. She gazed at the cityscape for several minutes while I studied her profile.

Nose, small and slightly upturned. Forehead and cheek bones, high. A well-defined jaw, but with a softness all its own. Full lips, enhanced by the slightest touch of peach lipstick. A faint hint of pale green eyeshadow enhanced her eyes without distracting from them. All in all, she was like something out of a picture book.

As if sensing my interest, she turned suddenly from the view and stared back at me. Then she smiled a lovely smile. She raised a well-manicured right hand and waggled her four fingers at me.

Before I could move or say anything, she turned and ran down the length of the observation deck. I took a few faltering steps in an attempt to follow her but stopped suddenly.

From the shadow cast by the observation lounge, a man stepped forward, blocking her path. He was of average height, well built, with broad shoulders and a hard, square jawline. Dark glasses obscured the rest of his facial features, and his blond crew cut was flawless. He wore gray dress slacks, a white turtleneck, and a black sport coat.

The object of my interest stopped quickly and glared up at him. He sighed, pulled back the cuff of his jacket, and pointed at his wristwatch. The girl gave a shrug of defeat, tossed her long auburn hair, and turned to the door leading into the observation lounge. He followed a few steps behind. I followed, too, reaching the doorway in time to see them being joined by a black-haired man of equal dress and demeanor.

The new arrival pushed the elevator button, and the doors slid open. I watched from the open doorway as the girl preceded them into the elevator. She stood in the center of the group, flanked by a man on either side. As the doors began to close, she looked up and saw me. She smiled that wonderful smile again, raised her hand, and gave me the same cute wave from earlier. I started to raise my hand, but the elevator doors slid firmly shut.

Spring 1965

It was April, and the old adage about spring showers was in full force. At least they were scattered, not the continuous downpour they could have been.

Maureen Rothsburg, my girlfriend of the moment, had come into town to meet me for dinner and a show. We had been dating for nearly a year, and I was excited to see her. Of course, she arrived earlier than expected. There was shopping to be done before our evening together could get under way.

I held up my hand, and a taxi stopped suddenly in front of my apartment building. I opened the rear door and helped Maureen into the back seat. Once she was settled, I joined her.

"Where to?" The taxi driver's voice was brusque and impatient.

I held up my hand. "Give us a second." I looked at Maureen. "Where are we going?"

Maureen was busy looking into her compact's mirror and smoothing her eyeshadow. "I really need to go to Charles of the Ritz for some foundation powder." She looked at me and smiled. "If that's all right with you."

I leaned over the back of the front seat. "Charles of the Ritz."

The driver threw the cab in gear and pulled out into the traffic.

As I settled back in my seat, Maureen grasped my hand. "I hope you won't be sorry for agreeing."

"Why would I be sorry?"

"The foundation powder . . . they have to determine the blend that is best for my skin tone, and then they have to mix it . . . while we wait." She leaned her head against my shoulder. "I hope you don't mind. It may take a while."

I laughed. "Don't worry. We have plenty of time before our dinner reservation."

The taxi wound its way through the crowded streets, heading downtown, then across town to 5th Avenue. The driver turned left to bring us directly to the front door of Charles of the Ritz. Of course, all the parking spots were filled, but the cab driver pulled up as close as he could get.

Fortunately, the rain had abated for a while. I paid the fare and jumped out of the cab, holding the door for Maureen. Our direct route was blocked by a black Lincoln Continental Mark IV Town Car, but we jumped the puddles and finally gained the sidewalk. Maureen was laughing by this time. I reached out and pulled her toward me. I smiled down at her and then kissed her firmly on the lips. She returned the kiss with fervor.

As we parted, I noticed a man in a black trench coat leaning against the Town Car. He was smoking a cigarette and, for some reason, seemed familiar. I discarded the impression and walked with Maureen toward the salon.

The salon's interior remained as elegant as it had been the last time I was there with my mother. The décor was French with plenty of mirrors and gilt . . . just the environment to appeal to a woman used to special treatment and care.

Maureen kissed me lightly on the cheek. "I hope this doesn't take too long."

I smiled. "It's fine."

"You can wait over there." She pointed to a row of Louis XV-style chairs arranged below the front windows.

I laughed. "Yeah, I've been here before."

Maureen squeezed my hand and then walked toward the main counter. I watched her for a second and then turned away. All the chairs were empty, with one exception. As I sat, I looked at the man four chairs down from me. He was shrouded in a long, black trench coat, and his blond crew cut was beaded with rain. For a moment, I felt a pang of familiarity but immediately discarded it.

Maureen was seated at the blending counter. I could see her face in the mirrored wall behind the attendant who assisted her. I caught her eye and smiled. She smiled back.

I settled back in my chair and stretched my legs in front of me. Might as well get comfortable. We were going to be here for a while. I sighed and looked around for a newspaper or magazine. There were none. Nothing that might clutter the otherwise perfect décor.

Oh, well, I would content myself with watching Maureen as she laughed and chattered with the assistant in front of her. I yawned, tried to stifle it, but failed. I stretched my arms out in front of me, interlocking my fingers and hearing my knuckles pop. As I recovered from the stretch, I looked at the man seated four chairs down from me. He sat immobile, staring straight ahead. Out of curiosity, I fol-

21

lowed his gaze.

The object of his attention sat at the counter, staring into a mirror as she waited for her attendant to return with her purchases. Her presence didn't register at first, but then I noticed the long, auburn hair. There was no taffeta dress this time, only a simple, gray wool, Vogue suit with a black velvet collar. The auburn hair was crowned by a simple, black velvet beret. Even without the taffeta dress, I knew it was her. In reaction, I stared at the mirrored wall that captured the green eyes and striking facial features.

I was transfixed.

How could this be happening? The first—and last—time that I'd seen her was over a year ago. Yet, here she was.

I continued to stare at her reflection. The same upturned nose, soft lips, and gentle jawline. She must have sensed my presence because she suddenly looked into my eyes in the mirror. I inwardly gasped as she smiled at me. After a moment, she raised her hand and issued that signature wave. I immediately felt weak and vulnerable.

In the next second, she stood, thanking her attendant and accepting the proffered bag containing her purchases. She turned, and the man next to me stood as well. He took a step toward her and waited to follow.

I stared as she started toward the door. When abreast of me, she stopped and looked into my eyes. Then, there it was . . . that wonderful smile. As I was trying to decide my next move, she continued along, followed closely by the man in the black trench coat.

I watched as he held the door for and then followed her out onto the sidewalk. I turned in my chair and stared out the window. The man waiting by the car opened the rear door of the Lincoln and took her hand to help her enter. As he closed the door, I thought she looked at me . . . but I couldn't be sure.

Spring 1966

Washington Square had always attracted me as it has so many. This day in early May was exceptional, warm with a bright blue sky uncommon in Manhattan. My morning classes were over, and I had the whole afternoon to do as I wished. I dropped my attaché case at the apartment and then hopped the Central Park West Local at 125th Street. At mid-day, the cars were not crowded, and I found a seat without much trouble.

As the train made its way downtown, more and more people came aboard. By the time it reached Rockefeller Center Station, I had given up my seat to an elderly woman with two shopping bags. At Rockefeller Station, several people disembarked only to be replaced by a fresh crowd that almost overwhelmed the car. I stood in the center of the car, holding onto one of the vertical poles while watching the flood of passengers vie for standing room. When the new arrivals had claimed their two-foot square of the available space, the train gave a lurch and slowly accelerated. The sudden motion, though expected, sent us bumping into one another. It was all part of the game.

The bumping was one thing, but the hand that suddenly grasped my forearm was unexpected. On the subway, one bumped and occasionally excused oneself, but one never actually made contact with another passenger.

I looked down at the well-manicured hand resting on my sleeve. The pale fingernail polish was flawless, but the hand showed no inclination of releasing my arm. I turned for a better look and encountered green eyes searching for mine.

She pushed aside a lock of auburn hair and smiled. "Hey, you. I was wondering when you were going to show up again."

I was speechless. I guess *shocked* is the correct word. I stared into her eyes and then looked back at the hand on my sleeve. I tried to smile, but I don't think my effort was very successful.

With a laugh, she released my arm and gave me that wonderful smile. "Sorry. I didn't mean to startle you."

"No . . . no, it's quite all right." I was stammering. I was usually comfortable with girls, but this one totally disarmed me.

She was as immaculately dressed as ever . . . no beret this time, but a tailored, double-breasted coat dress in a pale shade of ivory. A silk scarf in shades of taupe and ivory was draped around her neck and was anchored to her lapel by a brushed gold broach in the shape of a leaf. A stylish Etienne Aigner purse hung from her shoulder. Of course, her square-toed, clunky heels matched the purse. As always, she was a picture and appeared totally out of place in New York's subway system. Girls like her traveled only in Town Cars or, at the very least, in taxi cabs.

That thought gave me pause. My eyes searched the car. I felt instantly confused.

"What are you looking for?"

I glanced back at her and smiled . . . a true smile this time. "Your . . . your entourage."

She laughed. "Abbott and Costello, Laurel and Hardy, Tweedledum and Tweedledee?"

I joined her laughter. "Yeah . . . I guess so."

"Well, Rory and Stephen are ensconced in Lord and Taylor's lobby, waiting for me to finish lunch with my friend, Annabelle, in the restaurant. I told them I didn't want them breathing down my neck while we were dining. I agreed to meet them in the lobby by two o'clock."

She paused and laid her hand back on my arm. It felt good. "I sneaked out a side door and high-tailed it down to the subway." She looked at me and smiled. "Nasty of me, wasn't it? But I do grow weary of being escorted everywhere."

"Why the perpetual escorts?"

She laughed. "My father's idea. I've had them ever since I was allowed to go out alone." She paused for a moment and then shook her head. "Who am I kidding? I've never been allowed to be alone."

I was taken aback. "Why not?"

"My father's work . . . or I should say, our *family's* work."

"Which is?"

She issued a condescending smile. "Trust me. You don't want to know."

Suddenly, the train began to slow as we neared the West 4th Street Station. It was the closest stop to Washington Square.

She looked up in surprise. "Are we here already?"

"If you mean Washington Square, then, yes."

"Where are you headed?"

I laughed. "Washington Square."

"Wonderful!" She looped her arm in mine. "Then we shall go together."

And together, we did. With her arm in mine, we exited the car, crossed the platform, climbed the stair, and greeted the warm sunshine on West 4th Street. In a matter of minutes, we entered Washington Square with all its diversified humanity. Chess games to our right, kids with balloons on our left. Nannies with perambulators sitting on benches, enjoying the sun as their charges slept peacefully.

We circled the fountain and then slowed our pace.

I felt a gentle tug to my arm and looked at her. She smiled up at me. "Let's sit and enjoy our freedom." She led me to one of the semi-circular benches that skirted the park. Smoothing her dress, she sat and pulled me down beside her. Her hand remained in mine.

I watched as she closed her eyes and tilted her head backward. "That sun is wonderful . . . what an absolutely glorious day."

For me, the day was glorious in more ways than one. "Yes . . . it is."

We sat in silence for a moment, and then she slipped her hand from mine. I felt the loss immediately but was thankful for the short time her touch had lasted.

Suddenly, unsure of what to say or do, I stood and looked down at her. "Can I buy you lunch?"

"Oh, my." She seemed surprised.

"Nothing fancy, I can assure you."

She laughed. "I'd kill for a hot dog . . . with relish and mustard."

"Me, too."

"Then have at it." She smiled again.

I grinned like a fool. Her smile warmed me as nothing had ever warmed me before.

The kiosk was a short distance away. I purchased the hot dogs, grabbed a bag of chips and two soft drinks, and headed back to our bench. "Lunch for m'lady."

She clapped her hands in delight and, for a second, resembled a girl half her age. Her enthusiasm reminded me of that day at the top of the Empire State Building.

As she unwrapped her hot dog, she laughed. "A picnic! Oh, what fun!"

I handed her a soda. "I apologize for the lack of wine, but none of their vintages were right."

"Oh, clever boy. There's nothing worse than the improper wine with hot dogs."

We ate in silence, but that silence was filled with something I couldn't really define. There was a sense of completeness without the need for conversation. Yet, in our silence, we still seemed to communicate. When we finished eating, I collected the detritus and deposited it in a nearby trash container. I returned to our bench to find her withdrawing an Aigner cigarette case and tortoise holder from her purse.

She looked up and smiled. "Thank you for that marvelous lunch. I shall have to return the favor . . . sometime . . . though I'm not sure how." She laughed. "I'll have to work on that one." She held out the cigarette case. "Care for one?"

"Thanks. I have my own." I fished a crumpled pack of Players from my pocket and sat beside her.

She fitted a long, slim cigarette into the holder, and I hurried to light it.

"Thanks so much."

She subtly leaned against my shoulder as we enjoyed our "after dinner" indulgences. Damn, life could be so good sometimes.

Suddenly, she pulled away, turned, and looked at me. Then she extended her well-manicured hand. "Meghan Kelly. Nice to finally meet you." She smiled. "And thank you again for lunch."

I took her hand and gave it a token shake. "Paul Donohue. And you're more than welcome."

"Donohue. That's a good Irish name."

I laughed. "Not nearly as Irish as Kelly."

She pondered that for a moment. "No. I suppose you're right." Then she laughed. "But no matter. What do you do, Paul Donohue?"

"Journalism major at Columbia. I'm finishing up my second year. And you?"

She paused as she drew on her cigarette. "Well, I'm a bit ahead of you. I graduated last year from New York University with a degree in finance and business administration."

I was taken aback. "Wow. That's something."

She laughed. "No, it's not. I haven't been able to do a thing with it. I'm still living at home." She sighed and stubbed out her cigarette. She seemed to fumble as she opened her purse and dropped the holder back inside. "As I've said . . . my father keeps me pretty close at hand."

I looked at her and weighed my next question. Then I threw caution away.

"Just what is it with your father?"

"Well, he's protective to say the least."

"So I've gathered. Why?"

She looked at me, her green eyes suddenly serious. "If you're a journalism student, then I'm sure you know my father."

"Really?"

She sighed. "The press likes to refer to him as Boss Kelly." She paused to let that sink in.

"Oh, shit." I was momentarily flabbergasted. "Boss Kelly . . . the Irish Mafia."

"The very same."

"Hence the goon squad."

"You got it."

"Whew . . . that's something to take in."

She laughed loudly. "Oh, don't be alarmed. The press paints him as some kind of monster. He's not going to send someone to do you in while you're sleeping." She laid her hands on mine. "Trust me. He's not like that at all."

I gave a skeptical laugh and slowly shook my head. This information was a lot to process. "If you say so."

She squeezed my hand and smiled. "Don't worry. We will work it out."

Work in out? What did she mean? My mind was in turmoil. Here was this wonderful, lovely girl . . . the daughter of the Irish Mafia king. The whole concept frightened me, but it intrigued me as well. Now that I had actually found her, I didn't want to let her go. I looked at her sitting next to me . . . the auburn hair, the green eyes, the oh-so-soft lips. No. This was something I would have to see to the end.

She pulled up the cuff of her sleeve and glanced at the delicate gold watch on her wrist. "Oh, my God. I've got to get back to Lord and Taylor. It's nearly two. Find me a cab, will you?"

"Certainly."

I took her hand and led her through the arch to the foot of 5th Avenue where taxi cabs were always in abundance. I hailed one and held the door open for her to enter. Her hand was warm in mine, and I didn't want to let it go.

"Do you have cab fare?"

She smiled. "Of course, I do. Remember who my father is?"

I suddenly became desperate. "Will I see you again?"

She laughed. "Of course you will."

She fumbled in her purse and withdrew a gold ballpoint pen. Grabbing my hand once more, she unbuttoned the cuff of my oxford cloth shirt and rolled back the sleeve. She quickly scribbled a series of numbers on my bare wrist.

"That's my private number." She pulled me down to her level and kissed me softly on the cheek. "I will be expecting a call in the very near future."

Then, she gave me that wonderful smile and closed the cab's door. I thought I caught sight of her signature wave before the cab pulled away and was swallowed up in the traffic.

Spring 2007

The pain hit like a bolt of lightning. I took a deep breath and waited for it to subside. I kept my eyes tightly closed. I didn't want my memories to slip away. Right now they were still clear and fresh, but I knew that the morphine would muddle my mind, making it almost impossible to remember the fine details.

In spite of all odds, Meghan and I had made it work, but our courtship was far from smooth. Although both families were Irish, the Kellys were Catholic, and the Donohues were Protestant. Of course, Meghan's family history was a huge stumbling block. Most of my friends and all of my family protested. *What was I thinking? Was I mad?* Perhaps I was.

Still, we persisted and were finally married in the spring of 1970. By then, I had gained a position with *The New Yorker* and was making a respectable living. I loved the work and had continued there until the cancer began to hamper my performance.

Meghan never did pursue her career. Financially, there was little need for her to work and once our son, Sean, was born, she devoted most of her time to him. At the time of our marriage, we had agreed that we would not benefit from any of her father's pursuits, but that proved to be more difficult than it sounded. Although Meghan never mentioned it . . . and I never asked . . . I suspected that she was always there when her father wanted financial advice. The same was true of our son, Sean. He graduated from Princeton Law and was immediately hired by a well-known firm in Manhattan.

Sean loved his Poppa Kelly. From time to time, there were rumors that Sean and his firm were somehow associated with the family business. As a father, I found it easier to ignore such insinuations. After all, Sean, like his mother, was a Kelly.

The pain hit again, this time with ferocity. I winced, gritted my teeth, and reached for the button of the morphine dispenser. It was my only recourse. I lay there with my eyes squinted shut, waiting for the drug to do its work. Of late, it took the morphine longer to have any effect, but that was to be expected as the cancer progressed.

Finally, I began to feel a bit of relief. But I was tired, so tired. I opened my eyes and lay there, staring at the ceiling until I gathered enough strength to look around. The hospital room was large, accommodating an oversized bed and comfortable seating for visitors, the best money could buy.

The room was in shadow. It was night, but I had no idea of the time. Meghan was asleep in the recliner next to my bed, her needlepoint abandoned in her lap. Sean was stretched out on the sofa, snoring softly. My family.

God, I had been blessed.

I felt the pain slowly subside, and then felt of warmth of a body pressed next to mine. I turned my head and encountered a cold, wet nose . . . Max, my Irish Wolfhound.

How Meghan had managed to get him into the hospital, let alone into my bed, was a mystery. I laughed to myself. I guess there were some perks to a mafia affiliation.

I tried to disengage my right arm from the entanglement of bed clothes but lacked the strength. I wanted to rub Max, but that wasn't going to happen. I sighed and felt a tear run down my cheek. Good dog . . . good dog.

I turned my head and looked at my wife. She was still beautiful. Her auburn hair was streaked with gray, but she refused to color it. As much as I had loved the vibrant auburn, I was glad she had resisted. The color was softer now and it suited her as she grew older.

"Meghan?" My voice was muted. I was too weak to do more.

But she heard me, probably already sensing that I was awake. She sat up in the chair and reached out to take my hand. "Hey, you, how you doing?" Her smile was encouraging and as wonderful as ever.

"Hurting." My wan smile was no match for hers.

"Did you push the button?"

I nodded weakly.

"It'll take a few minutes."

"Yeah, I know."

Meghan left her chair and came to sit on the edge of the bed. She turned to look at our son. "Sean! Your Pa's awake."

I heard Sean rouse with a snort and a stretching of limbs. He dragged himself off the sofa and came to stand at the foot of the bed. He reached down and grabbed my foot through the covers. "Hey, Pa, how you feeling?"

I tried to laugh, but failed. "Not so swift, son. How are you?"

"I'm fine, Pa . . . just fine."

I gave a weak nod. "Good, Sean. That's good."

He came around the end of the bed and sat next to Meghan, his hand resting on my leg.

I gathered my strength and slipped my hand from Meghan's grasp. I held it out to Sean who gently took it in his.

"Sean?"

"Yeah, Pa?"

I took a breath. Speech was becoming difficult. "You know how proud I am of you?"

He tried to laugh, but failed. "Yeah . . . you're always telling me that."

"And you know I love you."

He squeezed my hand in response. "Of course I do. I love you, too."

I tried to nod, but didn't know if I succeeded.

Sean placed my hand in Meghan's. As she wrapped both hands around mine, I thought I heard Sean sob. It was probably my imagination. Sean was strong, not given to emotion.

I felt Meghan's warm grasp and sighed. God, I loved this woman! I had been so blessed to have her by my side.

I suddenly felt the weight of Max's head on my chest. That made it even more difficult to breathe, but I wouldn't have traded that moment for anything. I loved that dog, and I knew he loved me. I struggled to free my right hand from the bed clothes, and this time succeeded. I laid my hand on his shoulder and tried to stroke his soft, wiry coat.

"Paul?" Meghan's voice came to me from a distance. I was confused. Wasn't she sitting next to me? "Paul?" Now her voice was almost a distant echo.

I tried to respond, but couldn't. I tried to smile, but that was useless. I heard Max give a plaintive whine and felt Meghan's soft lips on my brow. Then I slipped away.

WIDDENDREAM

AUTHOR'S NOTE

EQUINOX is an anthology focused loosely on the idea of spring, and, for me, spring always makes me think of times gone by, shabby chic decor, formal women with floral names: the time of my grandmother. I tried to highlight my old-timey feel about spring by juxtaposing that against a modern backdrop for my story of Heliotrope, a modern woman but named after a flower and possessing a vintage sensibility. Though the action takes place in a Chipotle restaurant, our heroine is an old-fashioned lady, and the story's vocabulary features some old-fashioned language the reader may not be familiar with such as oscullable (kissable), widdendream (dreamy frenzy), malagrugrous (dismal), illecebrous (enticing), degust (taste and savor), brabble (argue about petty things), gorgonized (paralyzed), gyre (ring/circle), sonance (sound).

I hope Heliotrope's widdendream transports and delights you as it does her.

DP

WIDDENDREAM

Dianne Pearce

DESPITE THE APRICITY OF THIS particular midday, Heliotrope was finding it difficult to stay warm as she ate a highly unsatis-
fying late lunch inside a very malagrugrous and cold Chipotle. The
food, the restaurant's decor, the vibe, none of it suited her. While she
could appreciate the whole "industrial" thing as a thing, it wasn't *her*
thing. The walls were clad in metal; oh well, maybe it was fake metal,
but it certainly looked real. The counters, the tables and stools, all
looked and felt, *metal*, cold when her skin met their industrial skin,
and all were the color of the pinto beans in her bowl, but where the
beans were soft and yielding, the restaurant was not.

Of course she had to sit to eat. She wasn't a person whose un-
couth parents had raised her in a barn with the door left open. And
she was not, also, a fan of climbing onto multistory stools to sit at tall
tables and try to eat while her legs dangled beneath her like waiting
clappers. Dead, spindly weight. It was hard to keep her clogs on, and,
of course, Heliotrope always wore clogs, if for no other reason than
that she *had* always worn clogs, at least since the seventh grade, and,
in any case, they made a lovely horsey sort of clip clop when she
walked down any hall lacking carpet, but a dignified clip clop, like a
Tennessee Walking Horse, not a downtown carriage nag. Heliotrope
had always been dignified.

However, as she bent over the bowl of pintos swimming in a
vast sea of sour cream while seated at the high hat in the damn

Chipotle, the clogs, dangling at the end of her pins, involuntarily swayed and whacked one another, and the noise they made was far too close to the "There's no place like home" clicking of Judy Garland's exquisite shoes. Sure, Heliotrope would take a day off from clogs to wear *those* fabulous shoes, but she hated the whole, "Wow, you had an astounding experience where you saved . . . everyone! Time to go home now and go back to being monochrome." Clearly Frank L. Baum was no feminist. And Chipotle was no place for a lady to eat lunch. But Heliotrope was, most certainly, a feminist, and a lady, and a fairly illecebrous example of both.

Really, though, she was not here to cavil on to herself in a silent monologue about the establishment, and she worried that it was not good for her digestion to do so. She began to degust her meal, trying to concentrate on the positives, like the gentle texture and subtle peppery taste of the aforementioned pinto beans. The problem with the positives were that they ignored the known fact that Heliotrope did not possess a constitution well-equipped to handle fast food of any kind, and this was her third time at this particular Chipotle this week. And, as had happened on the other two visits, it seemed that wherever she sat, people constellated at the same high hat as she, which she found encroaching.

On Tuesday a middle-aged couple had come into the establishment hand-in-hand, and had progressed through the cafeteria-style line in the same way, only to begin to brabble among themselves immediately upon perching at Heliotrope's end of the communal seating. Heliotrope was somehow blind to how monsterful osculable she was, but the male portion of that couple was not. There was something of a young Penny Singleton about her which made many a man want to perform random feats of strength when in her presence. This one had been no different, lifting the heavy metal stools over his head and moving them into a different position, ostensibly to provide warmer seating for his good lady, but, though Heliotrope was blind to his ulterior motive, his good lady was not. Brabbling ensued. Heliotrope hardly noticed beyond feeling that she wished the world was a bit emptier.

Today's table mates worked at the local Geek Squad, if their shirts were to be believed, and, not able to excuse the hefting of heavy stools in anyway, as they were all male, and young, and equally able to heft the stools, they resorted to the lowest common denominator, doing stupid things with the plastic utensils, trying to attract her attention, and kenching and cackling and slapping each other when they had success. Heliotrope's eyes were fixed out the window on the dammed Coke truck that had been there as long as she had on this particular day, and she bored into the red "O" with her vision, trying to encourage it to move, and trying to block out the kenching of the men. She was starting to believe that this Coke truck had broken down, and would be there until the next day, and if it was, that would mean another bowl of beans for midday meal overmorrow, not something she contemplated with tranquility. The geeks eventually gave up on this lovely but unreachable woman, and left to go to their next appointment, or to Jamba Juice, one being as much the same as the other in their world, but they did wonder at her fixation on the window.

What brought Heliotrope to that Chipotle her third day that week was not the Coke truck, or the pinto beans, but was, in fact, the pediatrician's office just across the parking lot. Heliotrope was a lady, but she did not enjoy the lady-like employment she had held for the past four years, keeping the records at the local town hall. She found the work bland, scentless, without piquancy, and stultifying. To be among the brambles, the milkweed, the morning glories, that was the deep desire of Heliotrope. And so, one day she took a half a day from her bank of personal time and used it to visit all the locally owned businesses, and to ask them, each one, if she could design their landscape for them, on spec. The pediatrician was the only one willing to give her a try, as all the businesses used the local firm made up of ancient family stock from their little county and saw no reason to change: to hire someone new, to look beyond hydrangeas and peaceful bamboo, would have been considered radical, unnecessary, and disloyal. But the pediatrician, in some ways viewing Heliotrope as an adolescent who needed encouragement, and in some ways tired of the unspoken county rules, decided to offer her this challenge, "Impress me by the time spring is here with something astounding in the front garden, and you've got the job."

Heliotrope accepted the challenge, and had secretly gone to the office grounds for many nights in October, shivering in the chill as she gently removed turf and planted bulbs. The effect, when spring came, was to have had the patch in front of the door to the doctor's building bloom, just in time for the Easter holiday. The surprise was to be a double one in that no one knew that she had been there, and also that Heliotrope had planted her bulbs as if the patch was not just a grass plot of six foot by five foot and nine inches, but as if the flat earth beneath the grass was an Easter basket full of colored eggs. It could be beautiful, and impressive.

But here she was, trying to peak at the plot from the Chipotle, and here spring was, just two days away on her calendar, and Easter only a week after. She didn't think the flowers were going to bloom in time, as she had not seen even one minuscule crocus or windflower when last she looked two days ago.

Finally, her anxiety was interrupted when the Coke truck sputtered back from the dead. She heard the gears grind, and the behemoth lurched away from the parking lot. Heliotrope thought she saw. . .

Nothing! It was just a tern poking around in the grass, and then suddenly taking flight. It looked to have left a red feather behind on the lawn. Heliotrope was just about to dismount the stool in tears when, wait, terns don't have red on them!

She stretched her vision as far through the window glass as she was able. There they were, a little cluster of dark pink or red, a hyacinth, surrounded by geraniums, and next to them, did she see? Alyssum. She had worried overmuch about the seeds serving a cold snap a few weeks back, after she had quietly sprinkled them over the soil during a March midnight, but they had come through! She wanted to run out the door, to run over to the grass, part the cold blades, and see what she could see, but the site of the flowers temporarily gorgonised her and stopped her breath. When she finally was able to move, the best she could do was to fall off the stool, and wouldn't you know it, no one was there to perform a feat of strength and catch her. She struggled to her clog-shod feet, and ran, in a most unladylike manner, leaving her wilting pintos behind, out the door toward the medical office. Convention be dammed; she couldn't help herself! She was not in her right mind; she was giddy with excitement; she had done it!

Upon reaching the precious polychromatic patch she got down on her knees alongside it in the grass and inhaled the perfume of her zeal. She relaxed into the green grass gyre, midriff first, and opened and opened and opened, letting the dew of twitter-light fall on and about her as life spread its petals before her in a calamitous parkway of colors.

BLACK LACE, BROKEN FEATHERS

AUTHOR'S NOTE

For me, stories start with neither characters nor plot, but at an intersection. Not a road junction, but the fortuitous or deliberate connection of thoughts. My wife, Judith, and I were writing stories about the Vietnam generation for our collection, *The War We Shared*. Most of my tales involved guys who'd served in the war as I had, so I wanted to create a protagonist whose student deferment shielded him.

Thought #1: Vietnam had led me to a spiritual path on which I'd been strongly energized by "The Power of the Word," one of the Pathwork Lectures. Wanting to share some of what I'd been given became Thought #2.

Thought #3, which became the basis of my story, "Black Lace, Broken Feathers," was a complaint. Writing is a tough racket to get into, and I wanted to support myself at it. The brand-name authors always had a significant jump on unknown writers like me.

So I had three elements, each complex enough to wrestle with the others. No title yet, and I still have no idea how "Black Lace, Broken Feathers" emerged, but I liked its tone. No plot, no characters, but I could build them to fit the situation.

All I had to do after that was write the damned thing.
WFC

BLACK LACE, BROKEN FEATHERS

William F. Crandell

I REMEMBER READING BUDDY GREEN'S first manuscript, *Black Lace, Broken Feathers*, back in 1977 and thinking that an old pro like Emerson Hughes could get away with it, but not some unknown punk like Buddy. Which is why I was so stunned when, a year later, Hughes won the Pulitzer Prize for Green's novel.

Not that anybody else knows, even now, that the work was Buddy's. I didn't become the legendary Jonathan Rodegast, dean of the literary agents, by giving away information, or by sullying the loftiest award in the world of books. No, I haven't told anybody else this little tale until now, fifteen years later.

When I first met Buddy Green in the spring of '77 at the Byrdcliffe writers conference in Woodstock, he was the sort of character that appeared in novels I represented but did not enjoy: middle twenties, brash, argumentative, pushy even by New York City standards. I wanted to strangle him with my bow tie.

"All these big-shot, so-called writers have egos the size of Central Park," Buddy stood up and said in the question-and-answer period after Lydia Devereau and I had finished our presentation on what agents do. "They write one big-deal novel and coast downhill on their reputations the rest of their lives, pretending all they care about is art. And the publishers only want brand names."

I have no patience with posturing. "And your question is–?" I

43

prompted, a bit peevishly.

"My question," he smirked, "is why don't they just admit all they want is the money? Every writer in the business'd sell his soul for a blockbuster, and so would I." Buddy turned to the woman beside me on the dais. "I mean, Ms. Devereau, you're Emerson Hughes's agent." She was more to Hughes than that, but it was not the young man's business. "Hughes had one huge score in the forties and he's been looking for another gold mine ever since, right? Isn't getting rich what it's all about?"

Lydia Devereau was one of the early examples of how attractive a woman of fifty could be, her short champagne blonde hair perfectly in place, her quick blue eyes set off by a matching dress that fit her trim figure. She faced the barbarian like a British colonial governor's lady. "If you believe that, Mister–"

"Buddy Green."

"Mister Green," she said, her dimples savoring the double entendre, "you haven't tasted fame yet. And you still have many lessons to learn."

I never would have guessed then that Lydia would tutor him. But then, in spring young men go mad.

After the panel ended, Buddy Green buttonholed me and I finally agreed to look at his manuscript. If any of his intensity leaked onto the printed page, he could have something, I thought. Otherwise, I would send him the most scathing rejection letter an agent ever penned. How could I lose?

It was, simply, the best novel I ever read–a large multi-faceted emerald of a novel, about love and betrayal in the late Eisenhower era. How clever to have given voice to his boyish anger through a narrator his father's age, looking back on a vanished time! The insights, the images, the cynicism–brilliant, I thought, but impossible to accept from a snot-nosed kid who hadn't gone through puberty yet in those brown, autumnal years. No, I concluded, it would not do.

He had mentioned to me at the writers conference how greatly he admired Emerson Hughes, the former fighter pilot whose one masterpiece had been a sardonic favorite of Jack Kennedy's twenty-five years earlier. By 1977, Hughes was a dried-up oasis, his most recent work a leaden modernization of King Lear set in, of all places, Harlem. For the past decade he had vanished from view, his agent-lover letting it be known that he was closeted in his lavish Adirondack chalet to write the greatest book of his career.

The literary world had stopped holding its collective breath by the time I sent the manuscript for *Black Lace, Broken Feathers* back to the kid from Brooklyn. "Wonderful novel," I said in my letter. "I can see how Emerson Hughes, Joseph Heller, and Kurt Vonnegut have influenced you, but you've soared beyond them. I wish I could represent you. My candid opinion, however, is that no publisher will accept a masterwork from, if you'll pardon the mot juste, a Green kid."

There was no way I could have proved that Buddy Green rather than Emerson Hughes wrote *Black Lace, Broken Feathers*. Agents do not keep copies of manuscripts they reject. Yet I recalled whole passages of this one, the writing was that vivid. The haunting novel the upstart had sent me bore the same enigmatic title, had the same sharply drawn characters and flawless plot as the blockbuster for which Hughes was given the Pulitzer and the National Book Award the following year.

Even without that famous illustration of a majestically glacial blonde on the dust jacket, *Black Lace, Broken Feathers* would have made an enormous amount of money. It shattered sales records in hardcover, in paperback, and again when the film version won four Oscars. It was what the unlettered Cossacks of today's "publishing industry" call a good read, so pleasurable an assemblage of sex and adventure that skilled writing and lavish critical acclaim could not sink it.

The third time I saw Emerson Hughes honored for his "comeback triumph," his greying curls and Bogart grin offsetting the rumpled tuxedo he wore, I put in a call to the kid. This would have been after the film version of *Black Lace* swept the 1981 Academy Awards. It took three tries and a threat to expose Buddy in the Times Book Review before he stopped pretending ignorance. We met for a drink.

"Biggest sucker since Watergate," he labeled himself over Bloody Marys in a quiet little bar on Lexington Avenue.

It wasn't difficult to deduce what had happened. Greedy for money and recognition, *L'Enfant Brooklynaise* had sent my generous rejection letter along with his no-longer-virginal manuscript to Lydia Devereau, thinking that my high opinion of his work, rather than the writing itself, would impress her.

Unfortunately, it did.

"Y'ever see that palace she and Emerson Hughes have up on the side of a mountain overlooking Lake Placid?" he asked, stirring his third cocktail with a scallion. "No? Gorgeous! So we're up on this deck the size of a volleyball court, drinking Cabernet Sauvignon while the late March sun plops into the lake, and old Hughes starts in about what a good first draft my manuscript is, how much it reminds him of his own initial version of *Caprice for Violins and Fast Women*. Well, there was a big splash first novel, I thought." Buddy gulped the Bloody Mary and gobbled down the trim little scallion as if he were also at war with pleasant breath.

"Then Lydia says how completely she agrees with your letter, Rodegast," Buddy continued, his dark eyebrows blaming me for his decision to grease the soles of his shoes before mounting the high wire.

"She's still a very sexy broad," Buddy told me, as if I might have been too old to have noticed. "And she's wearing red silk and some kind of perfume that smelled like a countess in heat. 'You struck me at NYU,' she says, 'as an unusually honest young man who knows what he wants.'"

"I did know," Buddy pleaded. "I knew exactly what I wanted, and Emerson Hughes had it. Money, a gorgeous house, a woman as seductive and sure of herself as Lydia Devereau. Yeah, I'd have settled for that. And that weekend, I did."

I have often envisioned that weekend when the Devil took Buddy Green to the mountaintop and offered him the treasures of the world. In these fantasies I imagine myself in the part of the bedazzled young man, perhaps with a bit more sophistication and a bit less of his defensive cockiness.

"Wh-what did you have in mind?" the boy author asks, struggling to keep his Adam's apple from hammering out a warning of his over-eagerness.

The bright-eyed lady allows herself the faintest smile, just enough to form the dimples into which more seasoned adventurers have fallen to their doom. "You have sent me an uncut gem, Mr. Green," she comments flatly, all business, all understatement. "Potentially, it could be quite valuable, if it were polished and properly mounted. As it is," she continues, with a touchingly sympathetic smile, "you've handed me an interesting story that nobody would purchase. I had intended to send it back to you."

The aspirant sips a bit of Cabernet to moisten his throat. He is very close to getting what he came for. "But you didn't send it back," he reminds her.

"No," she answers. "I showed it to my dear friend, Emerson Hughes."

"Who liked it very much," the older man puts in, an aging fly-fisherman who knows one must wiggle the lure before one sets the hook. "Very imaginative indeed, I told Lydia. Has the beginnings of something very salable."

He lays an avuncular hand on the young writer's shoulder. "You know, Buddy–d'you mind if I call you Buddy–when an author, any author, sees a draft of something with promise, he can't help wishing it were his to finish, the way Shakespeare turned so many of Holinshed's stories into monuments."

The conversation has taken a loftier turn than the apprentice hoped for. He begins to see a garden wall made out of tidy green bricks, each of them a banded stack of dollar bills.

"*Black Lace* excites me," the grizzled novelist admits, and the fledgling's eyes dart to Lydia's cleavage. "My immediate impulse was to ask you to let me work on it and try to publish it as a collaboration. But my agent here showed me why that wouldn't work." The mother-goddess gives and takes away.

The throatiness of her laughter makes both men itch. "I'm quite sure you see it too, Mr. Green. As you noted so candidly at NYU, all the publishers care about is brand names. A novel like this with the name Emerson Hughes on the cover could be a bestseller. But with a photo of a charming young man on the dust jacket, it lacks both a trademark and a sense of gravitas. That is a sad commentary on today's reading public, Buddy, but we both know that the best you can hope for with your name anywhere on the cover is for *Black Lace, Broken Feathers* to be printed by an obscure literary press in Greenwich Village that will pay you in copies. I think you'll be happier with what I can offer you."

At this point in the daydream, I am apt to see Eve's ripe apples looking not unlike red silk stretched taut over a splendid pair of breasts.

The contract they signed the next morning referred to Buddy Green's manuscript, the "papers in hand," as "research notes" for an unspecified project of the older man's. Hughes and his lover paid $50,000 for all typed copies and handwritten drafts of the novel, and they kept my rejection letter as well. Buddy agreed to hold his silence, and to assure that he did, Lydia made him write a letter in longhand "resigning from the research project" on advice of a psychiatrist because he was starting to imagine that he had written *Black Lace*. I venture to guess that they burned everything once Lydia herself had retyped the manuscript with "Hughes" instead of "Green" atop each page. When I commented that Lydia was a tough negotiator, Buddy snorted and said, "Tough? She could eat your eyes."

Buddy wound up with $50,000, considerably more than what two top agents had told him his first novel would merit. The money was the only thing he thought he wanted. How, I wondered aloud, did that make him the biggest sucker since Watergate?

"It was mine!" he burst out. Heads swiveled all around the bar. "It was my novel, my creativity, my work night after night after night. I sold a Pulitzer, a National Book Award, and four Oscars for fifty thousand bucks. Hughes got $1.3 million for the film rights alone. I wrote the hottest book in America and nobody knows it!"

"And whose fault is that?" I shot back, seeing in his whiny child's face all the blaming vitriol that led me to quit the groves of academe in the late sixties, when both America and Red China were paralyzed by their Great Proletarian Revolutions. "Grow up, Buddy. Get an adult name and leave the generation of crybabies behind you." I was uncharacteristically furious.

People stared. It was Buddy who turned down the volume. "Leave my generation out of this," he snarled.

I had not cooled off yet. "Baby-boomers, you still call yourselves. Out of college and still soiling your diapers! Still brooding about a war that never threatened most of you, that's been over since 1972."

"1975," he spat, as if it mattered.

"Are you a veteran, Buddy?" I asked sharply.

"Not—"

"Because *I am*. Eighty-second Airborne, Sicily to Normandy. I proudly served my country in a real war." The images of a darkened C-47 growling through a starry sky filled my head, of a red light turning to green and of hurtling myself into the galaxy with a dozen black-faced farm boys. "Every time I jumped, there was a clutch of novels, pocket books, in my gear. I came home and finished college on the GI Bill with no complaint that anybody owed me anything. And then I–"

"Swell." The boy writer had heard enough. "Isn't that what you guys call everything? Swell? Pops, I'm glad they gave you such a nice war. The one they gave us sucked."

I was quiet for a moment, wondering if I had read him wrong. "You were there, then?"

"No, I was not," Buddy answered. "You're right, Rodegast. I had a student deferment. You prefer to think guys like me were gutless, as if it were no big deal at twenty to feel betrayed by your country and your parents for wanting you to fight in a pointless, vicious unreal war–an unimportant little rat-fucker of a war none of our elders had the guts to avoid."

I never understood middle-class kids like Buddy Green. What made them so goddam angry? Vietnam wasn't their war, they could get out of it. Riots in Watts were predictable, almost logical, but at Columbia?

"Everybody in this bar," I said ironically, "has heard these rationalizations before." Everybody in the bar had gone back to their own conversations and flirtations.

Buddy snorted. "We weren't afraid to fight," he said. "We faced riot cops unarmed. Look at the risks we took in the South. We just didn't want to be wasted. We'd have fought for freedom. But in Vietnam, the rhetoric and the reality were like night and day."

The naïveté was appalling. "Do you think yours is the first generation that ever believed what its father preached regarding the sanctity of marriage, only to catch him in bed with a whore?"

"I've read *Death of a Salesman*," Buddy muttered. "This was different."

"Because the rhetoric was about peace and freedom?"

"Because we never wanted to be just another generation of Johns."

The arrogant little bastard!

"Your problem," I commented coldly, "is that you sold out cheap."

"My problem," he snarled into my teeth, "is that I sold out at all."

That was more than a dozen years ago. Buddy's second novel was published with his own name on it in 1982. *The Senator Came Down Here*, titled with a line from a Bob Dylan song, was set in the early Kennedy presidency. It read like a sequel to *Black Lace*, though the characters had different names. The critics savaged it, called it "baldly imitative of one of America's great novelists" and described it as "clowning around with historical fiction." As is their wont, they threw a drowning man a granite life-preserver.

Two or three years later, I saw Green's name among the screenplay credits for a lamentable made-for-television movie about Lyndon Johnson. I asked some questions and learned that he had worked on a couple of sitcoms and one of the rewrites of *None of These and Nothing Else*, that pretentious, star-laden epic about the hippies that cost Paramount $38 million. Soon after that, Buddy began doing rather well–financially–as the author of a number of cheesy novels about glitzy sex in Hollywood.

Yet I felt a sympathy for him that I suspected he felt for himself. Here was this brilliant, angry writer whose first novel remains a masterpiece and whose second, had he been able to present it as a sequel, was quite good enough to have cemented a reputation of the highest order. A superb novelist whose greed and insecurity had cost him any hope that his talent would be recognized.

I had friends in similar fixes during the McCarthy era–though for very different reasons–gifted writers doomed to obscurity by their politics, having flirted with communism at a time when it seemed like a charity for the poor. A real writer has a need to write that I can only liken to the sex drive, an endlessly urgent itch. My leftist chums wrote under a dozen names, penning B-movie scripts, magazine articles, margarine commercials, anything to put words on paper. Buddy Green had been blackballed after a different kind of naively stupid act. He worked regularly at his craft, such as it was, and made a handsome living at it. But I knew that he was cognizant of what he had sold.

By the late eighties and early nineties I had all but forgotten about Buddy Green. His name did not catch my eye, nor did I hear gossip about him. You can, perhaps, understand my surprise when he phoned last month, saying he owed me a favor and inviting me to dinner at the Four Seasons. Whatever had become of him, I thought, Buddy still had a knack for catching one's attention.

He looked well, even mature, dressed tastefully–though it was not *my* taste–in khaki slacks and a blue plaid shirt with a red linen tie and a navy blazer. Certain of the curly hairs were white. He had the air of a man at peace with himself. Strange, I thought as we exchanged pleasantries.

"I blamed you for everything," he laughed, as a server brought Caesar salads to our table. "For turning me down, for setting me up, for relegating me to schlockdom. When I'm the guy who did it."

This was a new Buddy Green. "Actually," I told him, "I have found myself wondering whether I should have represented your first novel, or perhaps referred you to another agent. Did I sell you short, I ask myself, because you annoyed me? Would *Black Lace* have done well–if not *as well*–with *your* name on it?"

He smiled. "The truth is," he said, "who knows? Any of the possibilities could have happened if I'd tried harder to market that manuscript. Maybe nobody'd have picked it up. Or it might have been even more successful–marvelous new author, boy wonder, all that. Or anything in between. If *Black Lace* had struck gold with my name on it, my second novel could have been even bigger, or the critics could have pronounced it 'Disappointing.' My career could have been exactly the same. Maybe I came out $50,000 ahead and avoided being a has-been at twenty-six."

I wondered whether he believed any of that, plausible as it seemed. Or was this how he kept from feeling the pain?

"You know," he continued, "I did keep a copy of my original manuscript, Lydia's clever contract notwithstanding. What did it matter? Could I have proved the copy with my name on it was older than the one they sold to Random House? No. But I read all 703 pages, side-by-side and line-by-line. The old bastard didn't change a comma, not one word. First draft!"

That had been my impression, too. We finished our salads in silence, and he did not speak again until his fennel-smoked duck and my poached salmon arrived. Finally, between bites, Buddy continued.

"You'll remember, I think, that I felt I got screwed." I nodded. The salmon was wonderful, almost custardy in its tenderness. "Then we had our conversation about crybabies," he said. "I stormed out on you, but something shifted in me. What if I had authored not only

Black Lace, Broken Feathers but my own misfortunes? I stopped blaming everybody else and blamed myself. That didn't feel any better, calling myself a chump instead of a victim, but it had the scent of truth to it."

I listened, fascinated, while Buddy talked about his bad decision to try salvaging his half-written sequel, the Kennedy years novel, instead of throwing it out and starting afresh. He told me how he had turned to writing for television to avoid being pummeled by the critics, or painted white by pigeons, as he put it. Then he put his fork down.

"You know what a spiritual path is?" he asked as if it were not a totally new topic. I was formulating a sarcastic response when he answered his own query. "A spiritual path is the crazy-crooked trail you sleepwalk on through your life as it appears when you finally wake up and look back on it. From then on, the way gets clearer and easier."

It seemed to me that the conversation, too, had taken a "crazy-crooked" turn. I have a clear memory of staring at our attractive blonde waitress and fidgeting with my bow tie, wondering for just an instant if failure had driven Buddy mad and whether I ought to worry. Ah, the counsel of one's fears! But to my surprise, the sense of the ridiculous that has served me all my life kept me from sneering. I glanced at my own history and asked myself how rational a progression it had been from paratrooper to professor to literary agent.

Buddy waited to speak until I was listening. Surely that change bespoke the possibility that miracles can still occur.

"I went back there," he said, "to have it out with them, the famous novelist whose reputation I had resuscitated and the bitch-goddess Fame. This was in April of 1986. I flew into La Guardia and rented a car, roared up the Northway to the Adirondacks, not entirely certain I wouldn't strangle them both.

"'If you've come to gloat,' Lydia snarled when she opened the door, 'go to hell.' It was ten years later and she looked twenty or thirty years older. All the heat of my anger and of whatever sexual charge I still had around her drained out through my toes.

"I asked what had happened and she led me to one of the bedrooms. Emerson Hughes sat in an overstuffed armchair wearing a dirty bathrobe, totally unaware of us. 'Alzheimer's,' Lydia whispered. 'The man was a genius and now this.'

"This was at first glance a more horrible curse than anything I had ever wished on the man who stole my Pulitzer. He was having a conversation with an empty room, talking–and listening–to a bunch of friends who remained invisible. You know how writers are, Rodegast, even impotence doesn't terrify us as much as losing our minds. I sank weakly into a bentwood rocker and just stared at him.

"His voice was like a younger man's, less sure of himself than when I met him before. 'I keep telling her,' he complained, 'that I don't really want to be a famous writer, just a good one.' Lydia scowled and whispered that he kept replaying this theme, based on an argument she and Hughes had had in 1951.

"Then something changed for a few moments. He noticed me and came back into the present. 'Is that you, Buddy?' he asked. 'Well, isn't it splendid how well our collaboration has done?' He went on for a minute or two, all fake heartiness and phony bonhomie. And all of a sudden Lydia and I were gone and he was speaking to the walls again.

"'He has those lucid moments,' she said dully, 'but they're shorter all the time. Most of his conversations are with angels he sees all around the room.'

"I wanted to get the hell out of there, just run like a dog with firecrackers tied to its tail. But I heard a voice–not hers, not his, maybe just in my head–saying *Writers hear things other people do not.* I sat down again and watched him. Then I finally stood up and put my arm gently around the spent woman whose fate it was to love Emerson Hughes.

"Here was a masterful novelist who had been cursed by impossible expectations, a man who loved to write and was crippled by demands to keep outdoing everything he had done. His deal with the Devil predated mine by a quarter of a century. I wondered if mine had an escape clause.

"But I saw two things in that room that saved me, Rodegast. The first was that what Lydia Devereau called Hughes's 'lucid moments' were the ones in which he was all mask again, and what she thought of as his lapses were those in which he was genuine after so many years. And seeing that gave me a fleeting glimpse of what he saw in that room. I hugged Lydia and left."

The waitress cleared away our plates and took our order for coffee. I was still digesting the story of poor Hughes's infirmity, quite astounded because Lydia Devereau had just sold another manuscript with his name on it to Random House. Well, nobody ever said Lydia was frail.

By the time the blonde had refilled our cups, Buddy had told me about his spiritual studies, how he had told a former girlfriend about Hughes and the angels, how literally she took it. The next thing Buddy knew he was reading books and lectures, "channeled" writings purporting to be the work of spirits.

"I thought they were phony as hell," he told me. "I imagined these little old ladies who made this stuff up and either lied about the supernatural parts of it or–more embarrassingly–believed it. But the material itself always got me in the heart, always made such profound sense, Rodegast, that I finally had to just ignore its origins and soak it up."

Well, why shouldn't you? I wanted to ask him. Anybody who could take a counterculture icon like Jerry Rubin seriously at twenty shouldn't have any problems believing in wise and benign leprechauns or whatever at forty.

But what I said instead was, "We wore badges in the airborne, Buddy. Ever see them? Parachutes with angel wings. We were very young, so we joked about what was too serious to simply talk about, like love and death and blowing people's brains out. We kidded around about the angel wings saving us if the riggers packed the cutes badly. Sometimes, I believe, we humans use wisecracks as prayers."

It was a warm, enticing evening in mid-May. We took a walk and savored the scent of the daffodils and hyacinths that crowded the sidewalk's edges. I asked Buddy if he was still writing.

He winked. "Is a rich pig's ass pork?"

What a gift he had been given at an age when most writers have no idea whether they're kidding themselves, Buddy said. Once he got beyond blaming everybody for what went wrong–Hughes and Devereau and me and the publishing companies and the critics and himself–he'd started looking at what went right.

Black Lace, Broken Feathers wasn't the first thing I ever wrote," he told me. He had written short stories in high school and college, though at Columbia he had devoted his talents more to pamphleteering, which was a good way to learn incisive, brief writing. Once Saigon fell and the war that had captured his energies was over, he began crafting a novel out of some ideas he'd gleaned from an all-night conversation with a middle-aged Trotskyite whose voice he modified to narrate *Black Lace*.

"Actually," Buddy said, "my path has been remarkably straight. I learned to write when I was young, anything from leaflets to novels to movies and sitcoms. I have a natural keenness and I've honed it. And I've never had any trouble manifesting money with my writing. Emerson Hughes paid me fifty-thousand for learning how to write a novel, and if I didn't get credit for it, at least I know I wrote as good a novel as anybody alive. That's worth knowing."

"True," I commented.

"So now I write just for the pleasure of it," he told me. "No gimmicks, no eye on *Publisher's Weekly* to tell me what's selling. I write from the heart and I love what I write."

"Are you showing it to anybody?" I asked him. "Because you and I know that despite your reputation, you are a magnificent writer."

"True," he mocked. "And since I don't care about the critics, it won't matter whether they hail my next book as more schlock, or deign to discover that Buddy Green can write. Yes, Rodegast, I'm showing my stuff. Let me pay back the favor I owe you by letting you read this." He reached inside his black canvas briefcase and showed me a hefty manila envelope. "My latest novel."

He handed it to me and I weighed it in my mind. About five-hundred pages, I decided. Not an epic, then, but a nice-sized book, something to spend a few nights or a weekend with.

"No sleazy dames, no bogus Hollywood moguls," he promised. "Just a good, solid story about a guy from my generation who thinks everybody's lost the nerve to storm the barricades and finally finds that the real struggle is inside. And the real victories, too."

I stuck the manuscript into my attaché case, and started reading it that night. Last night. The sun came up before I put it down.

And the minute I finished reading it, I grabbed a cab and dashed over here to offer it to you. So help me, it'll be the most powerful goddam novel you ever publish.

THE ADMIRAL AND THE WHITE MULBERRY

AUTHOR'S NOTE

Several years ago, I was gathering up boxes of photos and assorted albums of pictures that I had taken from my mother's house after she died. I felt that beyond anything else, these photographs documented our lives. When I showed them to friends and other family members, their reactions were all different and not actually what I thought I saw. This gave me pause.

Within the boxes of photos that I found was one of the white mulberry tree that stood in front of my childhood home. Its branches and leaves stood stark against the backdrop of cement and brick. Its white, painted bark resembled a straitjacket surrounding its life and leaves.

Randomly, I pulled another photo—this one from 1958. My brother and I tumbling out of our room on the very Christmas that we got a new Admiral television as our family gift. The universe pointed out the contrast. It was clear that I needed to document this event and its impact on life as I knew it, so I would tell my truth and not leave it to a photograph.

Pictures do tell a thousand words, just all not in the direction we need them to go.

MAP

THE ADMIRAL AND THE WHITE MULBERRY

Mark Alan Polo

THE WINTER OF 1959 WAS unlike any that I had experienced in all of my previous seven years. Looking back, though the number of days remained unchanged year after year, winter seemed to last longer then, with harsher blasts of cold, deeper sweeps of snow, and a thicker darkness. And although I didn't know that when the equinox ushered in the darkest of days and longest of nights, it also would usher in a cycle of change for me that would alter the course of my life forever, and the life of my family.

We lived in the small New Jersey town of West New York. It was as simple a town as the name implied. It was west of New York City and it held a densely crowded mix of stores, brick row houses, and remnants of its past lives dating back to the late 1700s. We rented the upstairs floor of one of the many attached two-family houses built in the 1930s that spanned our block, sixty-third street, though the older residents always referred to it as old nineteenth street. The close proximity to our neighbors provided an ongoing connection. Secrets were as thin as the walls that separated us. Daily interactions, comings and goings, rumors and arguments were all fair game. We heard each other through our walls and reported what we learned to the other end of the chain by the close of day.

Ours was a microcosm of civilization that included a variety of ethnicities and religious beliefs, a fair mix of short and tall, thin and stout, good and rotten, young and old. But each night, when the rumors and neighborhood news had quieted, the evening pause and

59

silence was broken by the sound of mystery stories transmitted via invisible airwaves. The dramatic tableaus unfolded from the speaker of every family radio on the block. These were the only times when all family conversation ceased. The radio dramas provided the dialogue, and we were virtual artists, illustrating the tales in our minds.

We were almost untouched as a neighborhood by the first introduction to the television. A smattering of the screens, somewhat larger than today's smart phones, sat atop the huge speakers of the passing interest of the radio. Although not poor, or at least unaware of it, my neighborhood was a step or two behind the newest and best of anything. We owned old radios, second-generation televisions, cars from the forties and early fifties. Mothers wore their Easter dresses from years previous. Dads dressed in suits brushed clean of mothball dust from their weddings. The rush to acquire did not affect us but for necessity . . . yet.

This started all before me and continued until the winter of 1958. Had you stepped into our home on Christmas morning of that year, you would have immediately noticed the perceived lack of gifts beneath our tinseled tree; no toys, no colorfully wrapped packages or shiny-new bike, no robe for Mom or toolbox for Dad. In terms of gifts, there was only one: The Admiral.

Its arrival was marked by an oversized red bow tied to the middle of our tree and a crimson streamer that trailed to and around it. Mom and Dad made the executive decision to turn piles of wrapped gifts that Neil, my older brother, and I dreamed of, into one collective family gift: a television. To say that it was pricey was an understatement. This was a gift unheard of among the occupants of our collective of attached two-family houses. For better or for worse, we were the first on our block to possess this new, state-of-the-art scientific achievement.

The Admiral resided on the wall between our kitchen door and the door of the bedroom Neil and I shared. Like any leader worth its salt, The Admiral captured the attention of all. Its blond wood, metal splayed legs, and tambour doors created the drama of live theater on opening evening. These doors opened nightly with a clickity-clack, sounding remarkably like a drum roll. In ritualistic fashion, it marked the beginning of the evening's entertainment and similarly would be

60

closed, like a theater curtain, at the end. Not only did The Admiral impose itself upon our small but tidy living room, it also captured our attention nightly, rapidly, and eventually, completely.

A tension took shape within this small and carpeted living room. The balance of importance shifted with the intrusion of the television with its stern metal legs and upright frame. Dad's prized possession, a clock, no longer took center stage. It was relegated to the back seat and placed atop of this blond behemoth. Its glass walls edged in gold, the clock twinkled as the horizontal dial silently turned back and forth, pushing golden hands past a dozen graduated Roman numerals. Regal. But, no longer the room's only star. Like the seconds of a sweep hand, changes were happening fast.

The TV demanded our attention nightly, as it crept into our world, and like good automatons we offered no resistance. Days turned into weeks. Our block was abuzz with the news that my family had this entertainment wonder in our living room. So it was no surprise that more would follow. One by one the upstairs and the downstairs apartments rose to the challenge of acquiring this modern marvel. With each passing week through the winter, apartment after apartment retreated into the solitude of living room entertainment. Silence settled in on our block like dust with all of the activity being watched from the seated position.

The Admiral dominated. The excitement of fresh-fallen snow quickly paled in comparison to the daily drama and humor our television provided. Our active participation in winter–skating, snowball fights, sledding–turned to passive viewing. Neil and I watched the winter through our parent's front bedroom window, while kneeling on my mom's hope chest, spinning like tops from window to TV and back again. Our hope was for a school snow day. Mom's hope was not the same as ours. She tried to explain why the platform we used for our winter weather reporting was a different kind of hope. I never really understood what she meant. I just assumed she'd gotten whatever it was she was hoping for and that this was the shrine. Little did I know that it was filled with pieces of Mom's past which, following her death many years later, I'd have to clean out.

Our vantage point gave us a clear eye to people on the TV

screen and also enabled us to check as to whether there was enough new snow to cause a school closure the next day. The White Mulberry gave us our information. The speed at which the snow covered the bare limbs of our tree helped us to predict how much snow to expect. Like so many kids our age, Neil and I were ever hopeful.

As the winter of 1959 dragged on, it wasn't the snow that brought the uncomfortable cold into our apartment, but the wind as it shifted north and blew through the old windows of my parent's bedroom. The windows rattled their warning, shaking in their well-worn vertical tracks, pushing the chains like bells tolling for whom. We were mostly immune from the cold, thanks to the windowed air shafts that cushioned and insulated each duplex. But whenever the north wind blasted through our unprepared windows, we'd tap on the pipes that rose in the corners of the room. Our landlady, Katie, knew that the signal was a request to turn up the furnace. Within minutes, the hot, wet air barreled up the pipes with a sound akin to a boiling tea kettle with the croup. The raspy hissing warmed you even before the steam arrived.

Katie was attentive to our needs most of the time. When she wasn't, Dad filled in the gaps thanks to his ability to fix most anything. It's not that Katie wasn't generous, but she was overwhelmed. If we didn't request the heat, she would forget. She was a large woman with enormous legs. I imagined her sitting by the steam pipes that cut through the floors of the house, eating dinner in solitude while she waited for her husband, Vinnie, to return home from his nightly liaison with the A&P cashier who lived at the end of our block.

Yet not even the melodrama of Katie and Vinnie's lives could long hold our attention. Increasingly, our hours together as a family were spent huddled around The Admiral. Mom and Dad would connect after dinner and share filtered Winstons, breathing deeply together and filling the ashtray as their sport. As one, we silently stared at scripted life as designed by our blond captor. Neil and I would lay on the sculpted carpeting and watch the small black and white screen on bent elbow. Periodically, he'd poke me sneakily, just to reinforce that he was the older brother. We watched *Rawhide*, *77 Sunset Strip*, or *Father Knows Best*, depending on the night, and absorbed the drama and the problems that, week after week, were wrapped up almost as soon as they'd started.

Unknown to all, The Admiral set us up for disaster. Life was perfected on the screen before us. We watched carefully scripted shows that we thought mirrored life. Truth was, these programs actually created a false reflection of problem solving–dramas that were resolved across a span of twenty-two minutes with four commercial breaks for relief. With these timed resolutions, our lives became increasingly dull and uninteresting in comparison.

We became aware that our own daily living lacked happy resolutions at the end of each day. We were incomplete, as our problems were longer than The Admiral would ever allow. We began to notice that our lives were not tidy. We increasingly wished that the music accompanying the end of these shows would somehow supplement the end of our evenings. We were all left with a feeling of constant disappointment, silently desperate in the wake of The Admiral's bait and switch.

Prior to buying this modern miracle, we were an ordinary family that played ordinary games and talked to our neighbors nightly from our front porch with ordinary politeness. Before the black and white beacon of society arrived, weekends included washing our cars together with buckets in the driveway belonging to Katie's parents, or playing tag while circling Moe's '52 Dodge Coronet. We were always outside. In our pre-Admiral lives, we shoveled snow, hosed down the streets for block parties, and served as an extended-family to all around us.

The Admiral removed us from the present tense of our lives, as evidenced by the snow, which remained piled high at the corners of every block, no longer shifting from our play. Likewise, no footprints of little shoes wrestled through the onslaught of snowball fun. No snowball fun happened at all. Our response to winter changed as we grew conditioned and insular.

But it was the spring of 1960 when we changed the most. It shifted our lives on an irrevocable course of isolation and alienation from each other. As Neil and I watched the winter melt into spring from atop Mom's hope chest, we simultaneously watched The Admiral with such intensity that the equinox was just another shift in the post-commercial story line. I also watched as the first buds of The

63

White Mulberry made their appearance and topped the branches that reached for the sky above my front porch. I loved that tree as my protector and friend. It sat dormant from October until April, and during that time I felt saddened as the leaves dropped from the tangle of branches. But with that sadness I commiserated secretly with its trunk and limbs as I sat on the concrete stoop and felt the red and gold leaves gently sweep past my face before landing silently on the sidewalk. I would close my eyes and we would speak of the next time we would bloom together, where we would be, the stories we would tell each other of the things we had seen, the things we had witnessed, and the wishes that were fulfilled. We'd tell stories about what the future might hold. The White Mulberry was my friend, my attentive parent, my confessor.

Still, after all the years, ours was the only White Mulberry on the block. In fact, it was the only tree that punctured the block-long run of concrete that stretched between a green-walled factory on the west corner to the eight-mile line of stores running perpendicularly on the east end. It was our marker, and it defined us as unique from everyone else. Even though we were the tenants, we pretended to own the tree with the whitewashed trunk and the house we only rented. Landlord Katie was quietly inside, always waiting for her husband's remainders, so ours were the personalities that dominated.

The annual metamorphosis of my tree was fascinating. Lime-green buds broke open into spiny sinewy frames that would quickly become the leaves that cupped the white fruit. I swore that I could hear the pop-pop-popping sound of the bursting buds from atop the hope chest. As the air warmed, it rapidly changed to catch up where we had left off the prior year. Every day when I walked home from school, The White Mulberry fought for my attention. I strode to and from school without trepidation or concern in those years. The tree was a silent guardian, watching me as I walked to school each morning, greeting me on my return as the spring breezes caught the leaves and it pretended to wave.

But The Admiral sat awaiting my arrival as well. It fought frantically for my attention, offering new tales of wonder and new stories from the recent friends I had made on the little screen. I had spent prior spring months under the umbrella of The White Mulberry's leaves, sitting on the cement steps that led to our apartment, gazing upward, imaging a forest of tangled nature and fresh air. So easily, I'd grow lost in the mesh of branches and leaves that bore the clustered fruit. I could hide in my mind and sneak away and never be found. Now, the siren call of The Admiral beckoned me from behind my apartment door. I began looking at my tree with a longing for a more suburban life, the kind that *Father Knows Best* offered. I no longer felt content with one tree. I wanted a grove. I wanted to live in a house with a walkway lined with flowers and a crisply painted door, like the ones my television showed me. I wanted a single-family dwelling, with more than a body's width of space between my house and the next. So many longings filled my heart as I'd sit there beneath the tree during the hours before dinner awaiting the growing warmth that signaled springtime's end. Until the leaves fully stretched their frames, I sat bundled up reading or doing homework with a cement step as my desk. I learned to add and subtract, multiply and divide, while Jane and Spot ran up and down hills with Dick. As I wrote my alphabet and looked up at the brightly greening leaves, I no longer saw a tree, but instead I realized a discrepancy between my life and the lives of the characters in programs like *Make Room for Daddy* and *The Donna Reed Show*.

Through the months of that spring, I became more and more disappointed by my friendship with The White Mulberry. My time spent beneath it grew shorter. I felt badly, as the tree did not speak to me the way it once had. It seemed to dim in its brightness, flowering and fruiting while I sat upstairs, devoting my full attention to The Admiral, watching *Beat the Clock* and *Who Do You Trust?* as an ache began to pull at me. My bit of leafy nature became just another tree as I grew older by the minutes of the sweeping dial of the gold clock. I felt the conflict and turmoil, from all of it, but I couldn't solve the problem. Suddenly, I longed to be with the people whose little lives were neat and whose problems were easily solved within thirty minutes. The tree, which had signaled our home, became a lonely punctuation instead of a beacon. I began to reject it because of its isolation and how it signaled mine.

There was little to do about it. So many of the events that would define me happened under The Mulberry, pages in the scrapbook of my past. I was punched there for being gentle and unaggressive. Those who would still be my friends played tag with me as the white painted bark was always home base. We hid Easter eggs at its base as well, in weeds that I once loved and thought were the spring flowers of yellow and blue. Cindy showed me her private parts under The White Mulberry while the spring sun moved late across the sky. Soon after, Bobby showed me his private parts, also at twilight. I preferred his.

Life had its markers for me under that tree of spring. I'd wait there for Cindy and her dog, Wrinkles. I'd meet Bobby later that same day, and we'd go off together, far away from The Mulberry's watchful eye. Bobby and I would find comfort together in dark basements and the garages beneath our attached homes. Ours was a secret we dared not reveal.

I longed for a simpler life, fashioning in my mind one with him, at eight; one without secrets. But in 1960, what was clear to us both was that certain things couldn't be shared. These were the things that were significant to me. None of these imaginings were shared or returned by the holder of my intimacy. The dalliances meant little or nothing to the perpetrators, although significant to me. There was no one to tell and The White Mulberry fell silent as our bond was nearly broken. I knew it even then. No matter what happened around it, the tree now stood rigid in front of me, each of us rejected. But as life around me loudly signaled something else, my White Mulberry had nothing to say. I was different now. Bobby was different. We united in that difference for a short while, until he tired of the relationship, not unlike Katie's husband, Vinnie, who dumped the A&P cashier from down the block in favor of the assistant manager around the corner.

I followed suit with Vinnie and fashioned a secret life at age eight, pretending to blend in as much as possible. Vinnie was better at keeping secrets. His were the usual kind–the kind that could be whispered about with only the humiliation of his wife with which to contend. Men secretly envied Vinnie, wives openly despised him, but everyone enjoyed the drama of Katie and Vinnie's suppositions. I knew that my dawdling would not be enjoyed, or shared over the joined porch railings with longing or envy. They would only be despised, as the stories on The Admiral led the way and did not speak to my life, my story.

Even then, I knew that my secret would destroy the family to which I pretended to belong. Thus, in that spring, I removed myself from my family structure. I coped—survived—in no small part due to The Admiral and also in spite of it. I depended less on The White Mulberry that stood there in rigid silence. At eight I held the secrets of an adult, alone.

The Admiral had many opinions, but none of them mirrored my daily world. Although I felt betrayed by my tree of spring, my blonde teacher with tambour doors, gold legs, and a vacuum tube heart also showed me nothing of the life for which I was designed.

Nowhere on the seven channels that were available could I find anything remotely familiar to my storyline. Fathers solving the problems of little league for their sons; mothers, dressed in shirtwaist dresses, cooking and cleaning while talking about PTA meetings and boasting proudly of their children's achievements; boys and girls, seeking and gaining the pleasure and support of their parents.

I longed for a kinship within all of the minutes squeezed in between Ipana toothpaste and the "doctor-preferred" Camels commercials, but found nothing. There was no mirror for me, no spiny frame on which to grow my leaves. I abandoned The Mulberry and stayed with The Admiral, desperately hoping to find myself within the stories and the merchandising, but instead only finding nothing for many years to come.

The White Mulberry had no power in this game anymore—nothing to say to me in support. I somehow created my rooted hero for lack of another avenue and it was my creation of it that ultimately disappointed me. By mid-spring we were completely separated and we looked it. I realized that we shared not a bond, but a loneliness.

We did, however, have one remaining commonality. Up and down the block on which we both lived, The White Mulberry stood isolated and alone. Its roots bruised and buried by cement, with a cuff of weeds at its base. Instead of a beacon, it exposed itself as trapped. I, too, buried my roots in the cement around me. I broke all ties with Bobby and moved my longing to the next spring when I hoped things would be different. I never dared for better, just different. I felt determined to have a spring that I believed was given me by my White Mulberry. I longed for a blast of lime green followed by the burst of spiny leaves that held the fruits of my life.

In the years since that spring of 1960, I've had many bursts of lime green followed by quite a few droughts and blizzards. The Admiral, not surprisingly, was never much help and, eventually, failing tubes and coils rendered it inoperable. Its replacement carried the stories forward, acted, as it turns out, by equally desperate and damaged people who hid their lives fearfully while spouting the scripts that kept them from their truths.

The White Mulberry continued to blossom each year, tall and defiantly proud in the concrete landscape that regarded it as more and more a pariah. Its fruit, once shaken onto a bright white bedsheet in the late summer and enjoyed by all, was eventually considered just a nuisance. We still shared a common plight, though, as for just being who we were. We transitioned from joyous to isolated to nuisance.

And there The White Mulberry remains today, still budding, blooming, and fruiting. Not unlike my leafy companion, I grew to the delight of some and the chagrin of others. I fumbled and stumbled, eventually discovering who I'd previously been, who I was, and who I would one day become.

WHAT'S THE WORD?
BIRD IS THE WORD

AUTHOR'S NOTE

Home is a weekend getaway. Sitting in the sun on my deck looking at the woods is a vacation away from the mundane repetition of work-a-day week life. Nature, both human nature and the elements, and especially the way humans behave in their environment, provide inspiration for my writing. I am an observer of Mother Earth and her inhabitants, and a recorder of my observations.

I alternate writing locations, the leather chaise lounge by the picture window near the holly, or the wooden kitchen table, surrounded by houseplants, or the desk in my guest room looking over the bluebird boxes along our driveway. An iced coffee sits beside me, further fueling inspiration.

This essay came while contemplating much about the meaning of life, the existential boredom of suburban middle age, and the fabric of coincidence. Frequently, I am witness to something I cannot explain, some near miss, some run-in with a person I was just thinking about, silent thought transference with my husband, surreal dreams that portend real events, a random memory or scent that recalls such. While I have no explanation for the physics of coincidence, I can say that the answer, whatever it is, is outside of ourselves. My writing is often about the awareness of peculiar goings-on, the weird things people say, the strange things I see, to highlight the other-worldliness nature of nature.

It is in our very own backyard, not in some far-flung place, where true happiness resides. It is in the noticing of small things, the new buds on the camellia, a hornet's nest in the eaves, a patch of moss by the birdbath, in coffee, that we find satisfaction. In such noticing we awaken, a transition from winter to spring, from fantasy to reality.

CSzK

WHAT'S THE WORD?
BIRD IS THE WORD

Carrie Sz Keane

WHILE CUTTING THE GRASS I noticed a dead bird in my red bird feeder. I already take issue with cutting the grass. Not because of the labor, or the heat, or whether we should even have grass in the first place, you know, because of the environment, and the chemicals people use to subdue the weeds, and of all of the rigamarole surrounding lawn maintenance while trying to keep up with the Joneses. I had never thought about the correct spelling of Joneses until then, because it is while mowing the lawn, of course, that we have time to think about such things.

My next-door neighbors growing up were named Jones and it wasn't until I was an adult that I learned that keeping up with the Joneses wasn't literally about keeping up with Dick and Betty Jones. This literal Jones family used to have a collie named Trapper that would poop on our back patio every morning. My dad started calling him Crapper. They named their next dog, a sheltie this time, Cooper. You can imagine what we called that one. The Jones family used to keep those green and yellow plastic beetle bag traps in their rose garden. As a child, I found myself obsessed with checking the weight of them, palming the bottom of the bag, feeling the crunchy and wiggling heft, to check the day-to-day capture. There was a smell to those dead and dying beetles that I can still conjure.

I guess I'm still, as an adult, obsessed with this dominion of man over nature, this slaughter and wrangling of the wild critters to keep our yards neat and tidy. I'm fascinated by the ownership of backyard spaces, our postage stamp gardens, our broom-swept patios, our birdhouses, our rose bushes and beetle traps. We push the weeds out to the edges. We spray and we prune and we cut and we water. My problem with cutting the grass is that I feel like I'm amputating frogs as they leap out from under the mower. It feels like mowing the lawn is a holocaust on amphibians and insects. The lawnmower is a frog guillotine, beheading the innocent invertebrate zoology in the yard I have carefully cultivated to invite the very eco-habitat I now have to tame.

Which brings me back to the dead bird in my red bird feeder. The bird was belly up, with its little yellow feet stuck vertically in the air and its tiny talons curled. I think it was a black-capped chick-a-dee.

The thing is, I have no idea how that bird got into the bird feed-er. The feeder is metal, with a glass front. It has a roof. The roof is screwed down tight. The food comes out of a small slit in the front which is about one-quarter-inch thick, at most. Clearly, there is no door. Not that a bird understands the concept of entering and exiting through a door.

I figured that the bird somehow slithered into the feeder and got stuck and died from suffocation. I took the dead bird to be a bad omen. Again, I struggle with man's involvement in nature. Feeding the birds, for example, sometimes feels like an insult to the birds. Do they really need our help? Not to mention that the feeders themselves are like an invitation for the birds to be eaten by our two outdoor cats, Kitty Witty and BB Keane. *Come, have a nice meal, just beware of the vicious predators under your table.* I read in *Science News* that cats kill more than *one billion* birds annually.

The lady at Ace Hardware told me that she is astounded by how much money people spend on outdoor bird paraphernalia, literally millions, perhaps billions, of dollars spent by backyard bird nerds on suet and feed and feeders and baths and bird boxes and special boxes and squirrel protectors. Meanwhile, the Ace Hardware cashier told me, humans are starving. Yet, we feed the birds for hobby, while we kill their habitats and natural food sources, like weeds and bugs and grasses. We lure them to our feeders, for the pleasure of watching them from our picture windows, and in the meantime, are essentially fattening them up for slaughter by our outdoor tabby cats.

I don't know how the bird managed to get into a metal and glass box, but I was a bit too freaked to get it out. I asked Jimmy to please do so. He was annoyed by the request and said something to the effect of, "You can get a baby out of a vagina, but you are too grossed out to get a dead bird out of bird feeder?" I am a midwife. He can be incredulous.

He forgot all about the bird and so did I.

For about a week and a half.

Until it was time to cut the damn grass again.

I asked Jimmy did he ever get that bird out of the box. He hadn't. "Which feeder is it in?" he asked. I had some resentment that he didn't do the one thing I had asked him to do, for Christ's sake. And, lo and behold, here I am cutting the grass again for the third time this month.

I walked him over to the hanging red feeder to point out the offending location. But, alas, there was no bird in the feeder. No feathers, no bones, no bird. Not even bird dust remained.

Now I was freaked out.

It was one thing that the bird somehow finagled its way in there. But seriously, how in the world did a trapped dead bird disappear from a closed box? I had no explanation. Other than witches.

So many figurative meanings come to mind. I know there are omens surrounding dead birds. I looked up the meaning. A dead bird doesn't necessarily portend physical death, but metaphorical death. It can mean the end of a relationship or a bad job. It can be a symbol for the death of one thing, but the rebirth of another.

A dead bird trapped in a glass house has another symbolic meaning. Obviously, it suggests an imprisonment of some kind, and all of the trappings we find ourselves enslaved by, like yard maintenance and mortgages and husbands who don't do what they're asked.

But what does a vanishing bird represent? What are the psychic physics to explain such a thing? I couldn't wrap my head around it.

I sat down on the back deck to read a book to distract myself. I had started *Infinite Jest* the day before. I picked up the heavy book and opened to the dog-eared page. Cooper, the neighbor's sheltie, had one dog-eared dog ear and one ear that stood straight up.

Now here's where it gets really weird. The first sentence I read, standing alone in the middle of the page and as its very own paragraph was this:

And then the matter of the dead bird, out of nowhere.

How do you explain these matters of coincidence? These phenomena? The matrix, the fabric, fantasia, God, serendipity, connection. Carl Jung would call it synchronicity—well, actually he'd call it Synchronizität. Events are "meaningful coincidences" that occur with no causal relationship yet seem to be meaningfully related. Disambiguation. So, what is the meaning behind all of this?

I called my brother in California to discuss. First, we share the passionate hobby of bird watching. He can identify birds by their calls. He used to stand on our roof as a child and call barred owls to the yard by imitating their mating call. The barred owl says, "Who-cooks-for-you? Who-cooks-for-you-all?" We can relate on these matters because although we are separated by thousands of miles, we are often on the exact same page.

It was 8:00 AM on a Saturday morning on the West Coast. I told him the story of the dead bird. About how Jimmy never fished it out the week before when I asked him to. About how it just vanished. About the sentence in the book. About how the sentence was its own paragraph and how it wasn't even a complete sentence because it didn't have a verb. About how the sentence had nothing else to do with the rest of the story. About metaphysics, sorcery, divine power. About the concept of physics of coincidence and fate. Can quantum physics and quantum entanglement explain paranormal phenomena? Am I witch?

"By the way," I asked, "What are you doing?"

He was listening to Blue Sky, driving to a flea market.

You're my blue sky. You're my sunny day. Lord, you know it makes me high when you turn your love my way. Yeah, Yeah.

"Okay, bye," I said.

"Bye," he said.

That afternoon, Jimmy and I went canoeing. We got up real close to an osprey nest, close enough to look in on the babies while the momma osprey circled above us menacingly. We took a photo. We marveled at nature. Humans aren't feeding expensive seed to the ospreys. They seem to be managing just fine. When we got back to the car we heard on the radio that Gregg Allman up and died.

"That's so weird," I said, "Chris was listening to the *Eat a Peach* album when I called him this morning." I thought of the lyrics to my favorite Allman Brother's song:

Crossroads, will you ever let him go? Will you hide the dead man's ghost? Or will he lie, beneath the clay? Or will his spirit float away?

I found in the song the answer to what happened to the dead bird. Its little chick-a-dee spirit must have just floated away.

WHAT I LEARNED FROM WILLIAM CARLOS WILLIAMS ABOUT LOVE

AUTHOR'S NOTE

This poem came to me, quite literally, in a dream, when I was much younger. I woke up one morning and wrote it down. Williams's lovely poetry has always spoken to me, and I have wanted to dialogue with it. My poem plays with "The Red Wheelbarrow." I have always been moved by the earnestness and ambiguity of the line, "So much depends upon a red wheelbarrow . . ." What makes the wheelbarrow so important?

My poem also gives props to my dad, who did indeed wear Brut cologne and save my baby teeth. I remember, when I was small, feeling like my dad loved me right down to my very teeth, a level of affection and security no adult relationship has ever been able to match. What is here is not the original version of the poem, though. My delight for the Williams's piece is now grounded by me-in-my-third-act, and all the experiences that have brought me to this time and place, and I think my poem is better for it.

DP

WHAT I LEARNED FROM WILLIAM CARLOS WILLIAMS ABOUT LOVE

Dianne Pearce

So much depends upon the red wheelbarrow
that I left sitting
in your front yard
like some stupid and sentimental mutt
escaped from the shelter just in time.
I'm hoping you will be my lover.

I got to thinking about this wheelbarrow
glazed with rain now more than paint
the worn spots glowing white in the dark, like chicken shit.
I got to thinking about it.
And you.

And you.
And it.

And I thought,
Yea, this would be the perfect way to make a pass.

The wood attracted me
trying so hard not to fray
where the metal legs and wheels hook on
trying so hard to be still vibrant and red
the paint reaching for itself over the spots where paint
is just a memory
like young love.

Like the reaching of these days where I find myself
tugging and tugging
the extra blanket on the bed
trying to tuck it in around my far-away shoulder
cover all my spots, take care of the material underneath
in the very same way as that valiant and threadbare coat of red paint.
And I hope you can appreciate the reaching and the way
after pushing the damn thing all the way
to you,
propositioning and
positioning it in your front yard,
I had to lie on my back in the wet dewy grass of this April night
chill down the exertion of my ramshackle muscles
before stealing away back home.

I spotted the wheelbarrow
in the woods on the outskirts of that three-mile-town we like to drink
coffee in.
And when I saw it sitting there
waiting for me,
fine-grained and splintery,
I remembered trying to learn to whittle with my father when I was
still a single digit,
a shiny new pocket knife in my right hand
a small puddle of blood around the wood in my left.

I thought I would never see the lovely knife again,
but I was crafty, so
when I made ready to grow-up and leave my parents, I invaded their
room in secret

going straight for the old Brut cologne box that sat on top of my
Father's dresser 'till he died.
Inside, oh boy, inside I found riches beyond imagining—
Single cuff links, somehow unlost,
school photos of me
the wooden nickels from the Longhorn Ranch—beloved cowgirl
restaurant of so many birthday dinners.
There were bits of old watches that my father couldn't part with even
after they lost their time
that lay quietly atop the object of my search, the prohibited pocket-
knife,
still shiny and so dangerous, a desperate character, like me.
And then, small and beneath the knife, secret of secrets,
baby teeth, mine, a complete set.

I took from the Brut box what I wanted,
and if my father noticed the reduction in inventory he never breathed
a word.

And so, when I was thinking of you today,
I saw that wheelbarrow sheltering in the woods and I took what I
wanted.
The Brut box and my father are gone.
Things disappear and are sadly seldom missed, the stream carries us
down-river and away,
and so I saw that wheelbarrow and I took what I wanted,
and in the waiting and patient old wood I carved a poem for you,
guy,
just for you.
I carved it with my shiny forbidden knife.
Right in the gut, the spot where a farmer would dump a load of
apples, I carved a poem for you, tonight,
and it says

So much depends upon this wheelbarrow glazed with dew
because when I see you, I am one pale chicken,
A dingy hen too scared to squawk too loudly lest I splinter. Too shy to show the
flashy red paint I still wear.
So here, instead, is a wheelbarrow

containing not apples but a Polaroid of me that, hopefully, the dew hasn't soaked,
because it's my birthday inside that photo, 1973
and I'm in my Sally Star outfit,
and there is a sparkler on the cake,
and there is a look in my eye that says I was wishing you were there,
So I am inviting you to my party.

Now that doesn't rhyme
and I know it probably wouldn't make it as a poem
except that for every period, the dot on every "I"
I carved a little hollow
and filled each one with a little baby tooth.

So now, like a faithful dog or a timeless timepiece
I curl up in my house
pull the threads of the quilt around my far-away shoulder
and watch the last morning stars, small and winking,
hold their dull white and dissolve into the spreading light
above your house and mine
as I wait
for you
to wake.

TRAIN WINDOWS

BALANCED MEALS

WRITING

AUTHOR'S NOTE

In addition to my work with the Milton Workshop, I have the good fortune to attend other writing events in my community. I guess I am a glutton for writing experiences. I keep a journal of the pieces I write during these meetings and go back to them for inspiration. I have learned that having free space to write off the top of your head and share your thoughts without judgement is vital to a writer's life.

The poems that follow are based on writings from 2016.
DDB

TRAIN WINDOWS

DD Beals

The lit windows are domestic aquariums for my quick
entertainment
As I travel the LIRR into Manhattan, the City, my town
I have always enjoyed peeking into people's lives along the
line
There are hundreds of like monuments to survival
Some are fading into the weeds, some windows are
boarded up, and some yards are nothing but piles of garbage
Others are painted with bright green shutters, Christmas
lights all year long, and piles of toys in the yard
The flat roof houses are my favorite, filled with old
Spaulding's and lost teddy bears, and one with a car

I mostly wonder about the people who live in these houses
How they choose to live in a monument along the line
I imagine enough stories to fill many writing books
But I always enjoy the ride
Moments in other people's lives
Just enough time

BALANCED MEALS

DD Beals

Each of your three daily meals should be balanced,
the home education teacher said
Of course I thought
She meant I should stand on one foot as I slide my
frosted flakes into my mouth
She meant I should put a plate on my head as I eat my
grilled cheese sandwich
She meant I should toss the onion rings into the air so I can
catch them on my tongue
These all seemed like good balancing acts to me
Which only goes to prove that you are what you can balance
For me, I can balance a few slices of bacon while
sipping my hot coffee
Bacon-coffee liquor I call it
I can balance coconut cake from fork to mouth and
not drop a flake
I can swig champagne with a strawberry in my mouth and
not choke
I will always remember my home education teacher for
teaching me the art of balance
Maybe not just the way she intended

WRITING

DD Beals

I travel through the recesses, nooks, cavities, deep wells
Small closets, dusty shelves and grey hallways
Of my mind, my identity

Sometimes these travels take me places I have never been
Places so familiar I can reach and touch them
And my pen moves ahead of my mind

I am always amazed at the adventures
My mind can find and my body would never consider
How nice to be in two places at the same time

I am in awe of my mind's ability to create without material
Move without moving, remember without text
Dream of what could be without ever really knowing what is

Maybe this is what Einstein understood

DELIA AND CONNECTICUT

AUTHOR'S NOTE

An active antiwar protester during the Vietnam War, I choose to write a novel and several short stories related to the aftermath of this divisive time in our nation's history. One of those stories, drafted while a resident at Yaddo, the celebrated writers'/artists' retreat in Saratoga Springs, NY, was "Delia and Connecticut." Several summers before, I met the late author and former Army nurse who served in Vietnam, Linda Van Devanter. Hearing her speak about her wartime experiences at the 71st Evacuation Hospital in Pleiku and reading her book *Home Before Morning*, inspired this particular piece of fiction.

I created my character, Delia, in order to explore life after war for a former Army nurse with post-traumatic stress disorder (PTSD). As a counterpoint to Delia, I developed a younger character, Connecticut, who had no experience of the war but needed to heal her own deep wounds. In bringing them together from their very different worlds and generations, I attempted to explore the intersection of disparate lives against the backdrop of spring, which I consider a time of hope and renewal–the antithesis of war. I followed Aristotle's adage about the purpose of art, "To delight and instruct." I hope I've been successful on both fronts.

JSC

DELIA AND CONNECTICUT

Judith Speizer Crandell

CONNECTICUT AWAKENED ME, HER FINE hair falling around her face as she bent over. She pushed it away several times but it repeatedly returned as if it were destined to do this throughout her life.

I was in my long white nightgown with its washed-out pink rosettes, more white-on-white than pink-on-white now. She shook my shoulders.

"For Christ sakes, Connecticut," I finally said, "Let me be. What is it you want—it's, God, it's—"

I could barely focus on the square box of a traveling alarm flashing the green neon numbers of 4:40 AM.

We were at her parents' vacation place in the Adirondacks. The clock was something she'd insisted that I pack and lug from New York City, along with three sweatshirts, jeans, overalls, tennis shorts, two pairs of sneakers, a flashlight, and a stretched-out black bathing suit whose bright purple, pink, and yellow stars had faded. Oh, and my camera. And on my pillow when I arrived lay a new pen and a paisley cloth-bound blank book, courtesy of Connecticut.

"What the hell," I finally said, seeing her Paul McCartney down-turned eyes turn even more downward. "I'm up. I'm awake. Funnel in the coffee and we'll go for that 5:00 AM canoe ride you've been talking about since we left New York. Damn, dawn in the mountains arrives early in April. I'm afraid it won't be five on the dot though. You've got to let me piss and brush my teeth."

91

"Thanks, you're a pal, kiddo," she said. "It'll be cool."

Where did she learn to talk like that? Maybe it was the age difference—I was forty-one and she was two decades younger. I know she saw me as an older, wiser woman, but that was bullshit, incomplete, not all of me, some idealized version that fit her needs. Of course, that's not being quite fair to her. I'm incomplete to other people, too—my mother, my sister and her two daughters, as well as the doctors I work for in their ob-gyn practice, which is where I met Connecticut. She was a patient with an inflamed pelvis. I had been nice to her—particularly nice, she said later, and so began our friendship, with her seeking me out because I was nice.

The guy she was living with—was it Alexander? John?—who was around nineteen and wouldn't lay off her, even with her infection, had finally left. She managed to look me up, and within one hour of the call was crying over cappuccino in my one-bedroom railroad flat with the tub in the kitchen.

"This is really neat," she said, between sobs, rubbing her long fingers over the top edge of the claw-footed porcelain bath as we sat at my only table. "I love the tub in the kitchen and the bed in the loft." Her sobs somewhat subsided as she settled in.

I could have done without the tub arrangement maybe, but the loft was great for rolling in the hay—now where did I pick up that expression?

Several years after I got back from Vietnam, where I was a nurse, I reconnected with a doctor I had an affair with over there. Part of our evac hospital unit staff. Blood brother, blood sister. When we were in-country, we made all sorts of sick jokes like that. We had to laugh because if we cried, oh God, if we cried and didn't laugh, we'd turn our hearts inside out like dead pink rubber balls and be good for nothing and no one.

So instead, we drank, smoked weed, made love, and triaged the wounded, walking to the OR through canvas-walled wards of screams, mopping blood and guts like washer ladies from Ireland, wiping front steps and shining facets like babushka head-covered ladies from the Ukraine, scrubbing kitchen floors and then putting newspapers down to keep them clean. You could read last week's news by sitting on my Aunt Sophie's floor. You could eat off my Aunt Kathleen's front steps and see yourself in her plumbing fixtures.

I was a blend of vodka and Irish whiskey, but I rarely drank them together.

That's another story. This one's about Connecticut, my twenty-one-year-old pelvic inflammatory disease patient who became intimate enough with me on one particular night of pain to get served cappuccino in my kitchen alongside my bathtub. And to reciprocate, she had lugged me into the mountains and then into a dented silver canoe on an early spring morning with yellow, white, and purple crocuses popping out everywhere.

"Don't!" I yelled at Connecticut as she tickled my stomach through the thin white cotton. What forgotten tryst had I ducked into Saks to buy this garment for—married Mel or bisexual Bob? I lost track. No, that's a lie. I obviously kept track. My record with men was really zero since Dr. Dave—David Clarkson, "Babe" as I'd called him, "Babe" as he'd called me.

"Twins separated at birth," he'd whispered into my ear.

"United in a cheap hotel in Saigon," I'd elaborated, and in trailers, tents, on beaches, and then even in New York City for a while. But it wasn't the same in New York: no imminent danger, no death dragon, no river of blood to bind us with bandages. Just pleasant walks by the Alice statue in Central Park, long lines at MOMA, and a quick glance at *Guernica*, but it was only a painting, not the war. And it was obvious Dave and I needed the war.

Now I was being tickled by a twenty-one-year-old recovered gyno patient whose wealthy parents owned a lake, at least this side of it, as well as the two-bedroom apartment in the city she shared with no one right now.

As I continued to drift into the unfamiliar, I thought there's even a maid to make my bed in a few hours, the bed I should be sleeping in, at least 'til some decent hour like 8:00 AM. This getting up in the dark—that's why I screamed when Connecticut came in and woke me. It was like an emergency room in Nam. Five-twenty-two in the morning, twelve-seventeen in the day, or one-ten at night. They never stopped. "Wounded coming in." "Chopper landing." No, that was over twenty years ago. Connecticut wasn't even born.

Today is different. Today I have the pleasure of a canoe ride at 5:00 AM—or more likely it would 5:30 by the time I get out of the shower.

"No time for showers, Delia. Just hop into your jeans, grab a sweatshirt, and meet me at the dock–five minutes–maybe a bathing suit underneath, you never know. I've got breakfast and matches in a plastic bag."

Faded stars, pulled-up jeans, zipped sweatshirt connected to arms and torso, pink socks, and high-top sneakers. I wrapped a pink-and-yellow-striped bandanna around my reddish cellophaned hair–next time I wouldn't let my hairstylist Jean talk me into a dye job.

Finally, I went to join Connecticut, who had shimmied, jumped, and danced around like a schoolgirl in heat to get me to hurry before she ran outside. She was so not-woman, not-equal in age and life experiences, I thought. There were twenty fuckin' years between us–I could be Connecticut's mother! But instead, I was her friend, I guessed. How the hell did that happen?

"So your parents own all this," I said, pointing back across the lake to the opulent main house we stayed in with its classy dark-flocked wallpapers and rich cherry and walnut furniture and crystal sconces in meticulously measured spaces along the walls. This sprawling piece of elegance was flanked by smaller buildings: the potting cottage, a boat house, her sister's art studio in an English garden, her brother's bachelor pad off to the side, alone with its own dock and a single green-painted Adirondack chair.

"Where is your family?" I asked.

"Oh, around, driving up, in Europe, Texas, looking for Easter eggs. Around."

"So it's just us and the maid?" I asked, grateful for the warm coffee thermos between my legs that Benita, all cheerful and helpful, had handed me after I quickly drank a cup of black caffeine-laden liquid while Connecticut tapped first her right foot, then her left. Benita also gave me a bag of grapes.

"Yeah, well, I thought Mom and her entourage might be here last night. Believe me, we would have heard them–loud, inebriated. But lucky us, they didn't show. So maybe they went someplace else."

"Someplace else?"

"Any place else. It's better this way. Don't worry. We won't drown. I know how to paddle. I have a Boy Scout merit badge in canoeing."

I looked at her funny.

"I stole it from my cousin in eleventh grade," she laughed, revealing her straight white teeth. Oh, that thin wispy hair, what would even Jean the Miracle Machine hairdresser do with that? It looked undernourished, unloved, that baby hair. I half-expected to see Connecticut's scalp through it.

"So relax," she said, as we drifted on the mist while the clouds floated just above eye level. "I've been doing this for years. I only brought the life preservers to make you more comfortable."

A moth touched my right hand, a pale fluttering thing. A sign? Of what? No, I would not do my maiden Aunt Velda's trick of looking at everything in life as a portent of something else. It was just a pale moth on my hand. This was just a canoe ride to an island. We had arrived on the shores of early morning and the world was particularly splendid, alive with rebirth and spring.

"Are you listening, Delia?"

"Did you say something?"

"No, that's the point. The birds, there's even a woodpecker, the ducks, the flies even, they're saying something and the quiet, it's saying something, too. I love it out here." More softly she said, "That's why I brought you to my Shangri-La."

Words echoed off Blue Mountain and then there was silence. My heart was opening, some deep alchemical arrangement they hadn't taught me in nursing school. A new feeling was being born. Maybe something vaguely familiar, from a pink-lipped floral time of little girl dresses and Mary Jane shoes and mothers hugging and fathers buying ice cream cones. I had a good childhood. It was what came later that was shit.

But this spoiled girl, I realized, possessed amazingly strong arms and legs and was blading our vessel through the water while I sat as Queen of the Nile feeding on purple majesty grapes with dark Columbian coffee in a thermos clutched between my knees and the ebb and flow of a lake that mirrored something stirring in me. If I would just look, I could see it.

But I never looked—not even in the dresser mirror, often clothing myself in shadows and darkness. The mirror was only an accoutrement that came with the dresser, all Mission Oak, nothing I would have chosen for itself, an oak dresser with a mirror. I didn't need mirrors. Yet, this morning I felt a fissure, felt myself stepping out of a golden egg through the opening while Connecticut paddled on. This new feeling? I was happy.

Connecticut managed to bring a checkered tablecloth feast re-
plete with silver candlesticks to this brambly isle of tiny purple-pink
flowers, silken green moss, and a fir tree that reached low and long
and friendly instead of high and out of sight and distant.

Our canoe bobbed calmly next to us, tied to a pine branch, as
Connecticut laid out the cloth, the still-warm bacon, the bran muffins
with raisins, the gold foil-wrapped butter squares, a knife, hard-boiled
eggs, and half of a yellowy bread that tasted like my Jewish aunt's
challah, my Catholic aunt's Easter bread.

"Connecticut, this is yummy," I said, and then I noticed there was
even fresh orange juice. "You've thought of everything!"

"Yes," she said simply. Her voice continued to grow quieter and
deeper, as if the voyage over had transformed her, as if the water and
the mountain had altered her in some essential way. She was wiser,
lovelier. Her baby-fine hair was now gathered back in an ebony clip,
her tight jeans topped by a becoming baby-blue sweatshirt with the
four phases of the moon on it.

I made myself stop evaluating her. I did this too much to people—
evaluated them out of existence. Stephen Field the psychologist, my
psychologist until he slept with me, said that I was always trying to
make people less than or more than me. First I would evaluate them
and then place them on a scale. He didn't charge me for this information at the time because we were lovers. He told me I had been
doing it to him. I threw his first-edition Faulkner at him, even though
he was right.

"I brought candles too," Connecticut said. "No need to save all
the romance for men."

I found myself nodding and smiling.

"Delia, you're my first authentic friend," she said the night I had
her stay over in my apartment after her boyfriend had just disappeared with a would-be rock-and-roll backup singer due to Connecticut's persistent pelvic inflammation and his lust for the dancer's ex-
tremely long legs. Had I told this woman-child about any of the men
in my life then or after?

What I remember most clearly about that night is that we both
ate voraciously from the plate of dry-roasted peanuts and sliced
Genoa salami left over from Mary Ann's going-away baby shower at
my office. Then I served Connecticut some Rice Krispies in the

morning after she slept in the love-making loft which she christened "the nest." I had lent her a ripped kimono and green plastic flip-flops, and given her a clean pillowcase. You'd think this was all a first-class ticket to Paris. In the morning, after breakfast, as I tried to adjust my eyes to daylight, she was smiling and humming in the kitchen, washing up the cups and wiping off the knickknacks, hardly a sign of her lost lover wound visible in her demeanor.

"Just lock up when you leave," I said, totally trusting this girl with a name as large as a state–why do parents do these things? My odd name was bad enough, but *Connecticut?*

"I took your picture," she said, as we began eating our island picnic feast on this glorious spring morning of promise and blooms.

"I didn't see you with a camera. Is it hidden in the thermos?" I was feeling very free and open, and considered taking off all my clothes and diving into the cool, clear water.

"No, off your dresser. Two weeks ago. It was kind of hidden in the back. I snooped around after you left that day and I was wearing your kimono. It smelled of you. I was considering taking that, too, but I didn't. It was a picture of you with a guy. You were both in uniforms leaning against a tent, somewhere." She looked so serious and worried as she said all this.

"Please don't be angry," she implored. "I never stole anything before." Except the Boy Scout merit badge, I thought. "It–it wasn't a steal exactly. It was a borrow. I intended to give it back, put it back. Soon. You both looked so–oh, I don't know, drunk, happy. I never saw you look so happy." Of course she had only seen me a half-dozen times at most, but she was right. I never looked as happy before or since that photo and Dr. Dave. But today held promise.

She continued, "I wanted to make you happy like that–I wanted to be . . ." Then she cried. Not like when that John or Rick or whatever his name left her sick pelvis, but deeper, sadder, less hysterical tears.

I held her and said, "I was in Vietnam. I was a nurse there, and he was a doctor. We were in love. But it only worked when there was a war on." I felt embarrassed. "Vietnam was a different planet. Nobody can ever do that for me again. Nobody." Now I was crying.

She pulled me closer and whispered, "But I want to. I can." My face was against her breasts. Oh, how awkward and outrageous we must look, I thought for a moment, judged for a moment. Then I didn't care.

The bacon was getting cold, I had spilled some coffee and all I wanted to do was be held by Connecticut. David's small figure with a green suitcase walking away from my apartment faded, jungle fatigues and useless surgery on shattered limbs faded. Death, death, and death faded. It was just Delia and Connecticut in limbo, alone on an island in the April sunshine. It felt clean and good and I could hear her heartbeat.

CODE RED

AUTHOR'S NOTE

My son, TK, and his fiancée, Kat, inspired me to write this story. TK is a college student and an avid video gamer, currently ranking in the top ten in the world and is considered a pro or semi-pro, depending on the game. When a company recently expressed an interest in hiring him to fly drones because of his video-gaming skills, it made me wonder what other ways proficiency in gaming might be utilized. I also thought about Kat's passion for chemical-free, uncontaminated produce and the prevention of animal cruelty, which motivated her to adopt a plant-based diet. I contemplated the possibility of our food sources being compromised resulting in mass starvation or potential extinction. "Code Red" developed out of that premise. Being challenged to write in the sci-fi genre during a workshop exercise, I decided to set the story more than twenty years in the future and create a perilous threat to food sources. I leveraged video-gaming skills into the possible resolution. Next, I researched futuristic forecasts regarding space travel and habitation on other planets as well as their impact on the human body. Lastly, I included elements of a love story, reflective of the deep devotion TK and Kat share for each other.

BN

CODE RED

Bayne Northern

"THERE'S NO WAY TO STOP IT," FDA head, Scott Gottlieb, acknowledged, "It's a fait accompli." The senior leader looked exhausted. His once bright, intense, dark eyes now appeared shrunken from the swollen bags surrounding the sclera. His booming voice had been reduced to a rasping, breathy, hoarse baritone . . . his broad shoulders in a permanent hunch.

"How did it get to this point?" The face of his newly appointed deputy, Dennis Sprick, simultaneously displayed disbelief, astonishment, and disappointment.

Gottlieb continued to shake his head slowly from side to side. "We didn't have proper oversight. We didn't put enough controls in place. Corporations like Arrow Duncan Production took advantage of that. The GMO industry blossomed–boomed."

Sprick observed the FDA head slowly wipe a teardrop off the side of his craggy face.

"The goal of the food industry was to create higher-quality produce and meats resistant to bugs and bacteria. The plan was well intended. The world would have enough food to eliminate starvation on Earth forever. Good things would come of genetically modified organisms–GMOs–more food, better quality. Produce resistant to bugs and disease. But . . ."

A coughing bout briefly interrupted and consumed Gottlieb. He continued. ". . . as we know now, bad things have come from GMOs."

"Why did people keep ingesting the GMO food?"

"The public were uneducated. They had no idea. They bought and consumed the altered fruit and vegetables. The animals ate the modified grass and feed. Then people ingested the GMOs through the meat and poultry products, too."

Sprick piped in, reflecting the extensive research he had conducted to enhance his chances of being hired for the job. "The bugs turned into superbugs. They're destroying every type of produce that exists. The world's water supply is tainted with the chemicals. And now, people are getting sick. The animals are dying off, too."

"Yes, Dennis. And the hospitals are filling to capacity. Hospital staff are getting ill as well. Soon we won't have enough well people to care for the sick and dying. We are in the process of extinguishing ourselves. People will die from a disease or starve to death. Either way, humans will cease to exist."

"What about the organic farms? Can't they ramp it up and save some people?" His voice rose into a falsetto.

"Oh, son, they tried. There was a big organic movement. 'Buy organic! Say No to GMO!' But it was too late. All of the organic farms got contaminated. The winds blew modified seeds over to their farms. Their livestock ate it. Their produce appeared perfect—just like the GMO variety, because they were modified, too."

"Oh, my God. It sounds irreversible. How much time is left for life on Earth?"

"A few months—maybe six at most."

"Can't we start growing food elsewhere in a protected environment?"

"Where? GMOs are everywhere on our planet and in the water supply."

"What about the Mars farming program? I read that it was started because they thought Earth wouldn't be able to generate enough food to sustain an overpopulated planet."

Gottlieb smiled at his young lieutenant. He had wanted the deputy job more than any other candidate. He had obviously conducted research and studied the recent FDA undertakings. There had been a few applicants more qualified than Sprick, but none of them had the drive and passion that this young man exuded. Gottlieb always chose energy and enthusiasm over technical skills and ability. He could teach them what they needed to know, but he couldn't instill excitement and commitment. That had to come from within.

"You're right. We did initiate the program. Our satellite pictures indicate the farms are thriving and the robots are still functioning smoothly—seeding, irrigating, and harvesting the crops. The livestock continue to thrive and reproduce. They are routinely humanely slaughtered and their meat is freeze-dried for twenty-five years."

"Why don't we go there? Or send someone there to get the uncontaminated food and water supply and start a fresh farm on Earth?"

"We haven't been able to send any astronauts to Mars for the past four years due to the meteor storms that have been crashing into the planet. We don't have a pilot with the skills to avoid the blasts of asteroids and fireballs."

"The mainframe can't maneuver the ship? I thought the computers could outperform a rocket flown manually."

"No, they can't. My understanding is the space team can't program or train a machine to handle something so random and erratic—it needs human intervention."

"What are the skills needed for a pilot to attempt to land on Mars in a meteor storm?"

Gottlieb breathed a huge sigh. He rubbed his large, calloused hands across his tired face. His bleary eyes stared vacantly out the window.

"Dennis, we would need Superman. We'd have to find a guy with an exceptional positive attitude—even overly confident. A strong ego—he'd have to believe he'd succeed. A risk taker. Superlative athleticism, superb eye-hand coordination, phenomenal dexterity. It would be beneficial if he was bright and oriented toward math and science. All these skills would be essential to successfully navigating through the meteor showers created by the comet flybys, the fireballs, and shooting stars. He'd have to fly through all of that to reach the other side of the Red Planet to land and avoid the comet dust that follows. We'd need a super human."

"I remember reading about the comet Siding Spring that barreled toward Mars in 2014 creating a spectacular, mind-blowing meteor shower. NASA leadership was sharp enough to save our unmanned satellites by moving them to the other side of the planet."

Gottlieb grinned at his young, earnest pupil. He reminded him of himself in his younger days—an insatiable search for knowledge. He looked down at the orange-haired, freckle-faced young man, suddenly aware he was developing a fondness for him. Then a sad thought crept into his mind. Dennis Sprick would not live long enough to reach Gottlieb's ripe old age of forty-three.

While the FDA head was lost in thought, Dennis moved over to the conference table. He pushed the button on his computer watch, transferring the brain and firing up his iPP, the new technology combo package that included phone, computer, satellite, and weather station and sensory capabilities. Sprick was an early adopter, always the first to buy new gadgets and quickly master new technologies. His iPP sprung to life, automatically opening itself, folding the tripod on its back to move the device to an upright position and lighting up the neon-colored screen. Sprick kept lightly touching the monitor and appeared to be completely engrossed in his work.

Hating to disturb him, but wondering about the cause of his sudden, intense concentration, Gottlieb interrupted. "May I ask what you're doing?"

"I'm researching types of employment that attract individuals with the profile and skill set you just described."

"Really? I didn't realize you could research that online. What are you finding?"

"The most promising field that attracts these types of individuals is the gaming industry. Video gamers. They're typically young and coordinated—with phenomenal eye-hand coordination. They're ranked globally. Some pull down seven figures from winnings and sponsorships."

Gottlieb let out a low, long whistle. "How can you identify the top gamers?"

"Easy. They publish their rankings online. I'm really interested in this one guy—at least I think it's a guy. He's been playing for over eight years, and has consistently ranked in the top five for SmartBox XIX Nimbus as well as Call of Mutiny for the past five years. He has a huge following. I've been reading some of his quips to his rivals. He's got a sense of humor, too."

"What's his name?"

"I'll have to put some more effort into determining his real identity—but his gamer name is GunMic."

"GunMic?"

"Yeah, GunMic. When he first started playing, he was Monob, but he switched over to GunMic five years ago."

"Monob? That's even stranger than GunMic."

"Well, he admits that he was planning on calling himself Mono-brow—but the match started and he never finished spelling it."

Gottlieb smiled and chuckled when he heard the explanation.

"Let me run this up the flagpole while you hunt this guy or gal down. I don't think we have anything to lose."

Sprick nodded in agreement. Then he began bouncing around various websites. Within minutes, he had Id'd GunMic as a twenty-one-year-old college student named Derek Fentz, located in the Phil-adelphia area. After blowing out his knee playing varsity baseball, he became a serious gamer. Photographs of him depicted a tall, muscu-lar, athletic young man with light brown hair and a masculine jaw. He sported a broad grin in every picture, his arm always around a petite young woman with Rapunzel-like hair and a curvaceous figure. In the gaming world, he had won over five-thousand tournaments in either solo or team play. Sprick was certain this was the guy they should call. He researched Fentz further, learning of his earnings—multiple years over seven figures—finding his address and sourcing his contact in-formation. He tried to leave a message on Derek's mobile but the voicemail box was full. He decided to text him:

Derek, this is Deputy Dennis Sprick with the FDA. We've observed your stellar gaming ranking and accomplishments. We need your help. Please contact me ASAP at this number.

After about five minutes, his cell phone rang.

"Sprick."

"Derek Fentz. I checked to make sure you were legit. What's up?"

Sprick spent the next hour explaining the dire situation the plan-et was facing from the GMOs—the probability of the extinction of mankind—the extermination of all living things on Earth. The presi-dent had announced that the US as well as the rest of the world was CODE RED—the highest risk definition that existed. It meant that life on Earth would most likely cease to exist within the next twelve months. Sprick went on to describe the farming efforts and correlat-ed success on planet Mars, the celestial threats of the Martian envi-ronment, and the United States' dire need of a jet pilot with Derek's personality profile, athleticism, and hand dexterity to undertake a mission to the Red Planet. He could hear Derek utter "holy shit," "oh, man," and "what the fuck" throughout his monologue.

When Sprick finished his tale, Derek responded firmly and confidently. "I'm in."

"You're up for it? Just like that?"

"Sure. It's about saving the planet, right? How can I turn that down?"

"Could you come to DC tomorrow?"

"Sure. I'll drive down first thing in the morning."

"No, we'd rather pick you up—8:00 AM."

"Okay. Can I bring my girl, Samantha?"

"Yes, of course. To DC, but not on the mission to Mars, obviously."

"No," Derek chuckled. "I meant DC. She'd be terrified to go to Mars—plus it would distract me."

Sprick could hear him grinning over the phone. He liked this guy already even though they hadn't yet met. There was something charismatic about him.

Gottlieb walked in, huffing and puffing like he'd run up a few flights of stairs.

"Everyone supports the idea of the gamer, GunMic, if he'll consider undertaking the mission."

His deputy smiled, broadly exposing the space between his two front teeth. "He's already agreed to it. He'll be here tomorrow."

Gottlieb's lips split open into a wide grin. "Well done, Deputy. Be advised we are not going to follow standard protocol. We are not going to put this young man through a battery of tests. We don't have the time. We'll train him on how to fly the jet once it jettisons from the rocket platform. We'll teach him what to expect when he approaches Mars. Then, it'll be up to him to outmaneuver all the crap that's going to be flying around the planet's atmosphere."

It took just three weeks for Derek to master the jet instruments. He appeared to be adept at maneuvering the ship. The NASA team kept creating more and more challenging simulations—every time, he successfully navigated through them. They learned that Derek had an interest in astronomy, having successfully completed numerous college courses on the subject. The team was surprised to discover his in-depth working knowledge of the universe—the newly discovered planets, the perpetuity of black holes, and the impact of gravitational forces. He also appeared to be a whiz at math. His knowledge base and quantitative aptitude would serve him well on his solo trip to Mars.

His girlfriend always met him at the simulation pod after his training sessions. Upon exiting the facility, it took Derek's eyes a few minutes to adjust to the bright outdoors after spending four rigorous hours in the darkness of the navigation chamber. When he could clearly see Samantha, he called out, "Hey, Snu . . . I mean, Pumpkin. I need a kiss as a reward for all that maneuvering of the ship and missing every meteor!"

Samantha, always willing to oblige, walked up to him and lightly kissed his full lips.

"Oh, Peewee, I meant a real kiss after all that hard work!" He lifted his petite, five-foot-one girl off the ground and planted a big, wet kiss over her mouth, gently sliding his tongue in the small opening between her lips.

She pushed him back with both arms, feigning horrification. "Derek–not in public!"

"Sorry, Snu. I couldn't help myself."

She kissed him lightly on the cheek, then held up a green, Earth-friendly, food container. "I made your favorite lunch; tofu tacos with spiraled tri-color peppers and kale coleslaw."

"My absolute favorite!" Derek picked her up and swung her around in a circle with her feet dangling a foot off the ground.

Samantha had adopted an organic, plant-based diet at a young age and had avoided GMOs until that produce became contaminated, too. Derek had intermittently practiced plant-based, too. It appeared to have had a positive impact on their health as neither of them had succumbed to the intestinal distress caused by the genetically modified organisms.

Derek looked down at Samantha. "Aww, Snu, is that a tear on your cheek?" He gently wiped it away.

"I love you. I'm so worried you won't return to Earth. If I never see you again, my heart will be broken." Another tear appeared in the corner of her eyes, welled up and began rolling down her face.

"I'm doing this for you, Snu! I know how important healthy food is to you. I'm going to make sure you'll have that for the rest of your life!"

They stood holding each other in a tight embrace. Derek's chin resting softly on the top of Samantha's head. A tear escaped from his eye, rolling down and landing in her thick, wavy, tawny-colored hair.

She looked up. Her light caramel-colored eyes bore into his. "I love you. They chose the right man. You're the guy who can save the planet."

They remained in their embrace as technicians and scientists exited the simulation station. It was bitter sweet to gaze at the couple, so obviously in love, when so much was at stake.

Prior missions had taken eighteen months to reach Mars, but technology had vastly improved and working knowledge of space had expanded exponentially. Derek could reach Mars in thirty days. Mission planners estimated one week to load the cargo ship with the uncontaminated food as well as a few livestock and a supply of water. The ship would be much heavier coming back. It would take approximately forty-five days to fly home. An additional fifteen days were calculated to accommodate for the extra weight and to allow for the wider orbit of the return flight to avoid the ring of meteor showers. Scientists had figured how to avoid the showers on the return flight—but the ship had to navigate through them to reach the Red Planet.

The rocket was set to launch carrying the jetliner for Mars on January 1, 2042. If Derek was successful, he would return to Earth in late March. Many people and animals would have died by then—but it was estimated there would be enough living to keep the species going—at least the human species.

The navigation programmers decided to utilize a trans-Earth injection maneuver to launch the ship into space. The rocket successfully fired, catapulting the vessel into orbit without incident. Derek was placed into cyber-sleep and would remain in this state until the jet detached from the rocket as it entered the Mars atmosphere. He would assume control of the ship twenty-four hours after waking.

The ship was equipped with the most technologically advanced computer system, Female Emulator MANET, or FEM. Studies had determined that the emotional sensitivity and high level of empathy of the human female gender soothed and calmed astronauts under extended periods of stress. Scientists had been able to build the feminine emotional intelligence into the computer systems, enabling them to identify rising anxiety and tension of the ship's inhabitants. They were programmed to reduce or eliminate a crew member's negative feelings through empathy, encouragement, and proposed coping strategies. The MANET was a type of ad hoc network that enabled FEM to change locations and reconfigure herself on the fly using wireless connections to join other networks. The feminine voice was also determined to be more soothing than a male's, particularly when an astronaut was nervous under pressure. This discovery resulted in all spaceship computers being installed or converted to a female voice.

FEM spoke softly and sweetly. *"Derek, it's time to wake up. Twenty-four hours to reach aerospace of destination planet, Mars."*

Derek's eyes fluttered open. He felt super groggy. He remained lying down, rubbing his eyes, flexing and stretching his muscles, trying to orient himself. As consciousness returned, he remembered the steps he was to follow to bring himself fully awake. After about twenty minutes, he swung his legs over the side of his sleep chamber. He slowly stood up, still holding onto the side of the pod. He felt weak and wobbly. He stood, attached to his sleep station for another thirty minutes. Then, he let go and took a few steps and was soon weaving through the cabin like a drunken soldier.

FEM's honeyed voice interrupted his concentration. *"Well done, Derek. The imbalance you feel will subside shortly."*

"Thanks, FEM. I feel like I've been boozing it up in that bed bunk," Derek croaked in a dry and raspy voice.

"Simulated alcohol is not provided in the sleeping station."

"Oh, FEM, you always take things so seriously. They need to add a sense of humor to your program."

FEM sighed.

Derek continued down the hallway, bouncing back and forth against the opposing walls as he headed for the mess hall. He could feel his senses activating. After drinking volumes of water, consuming some sustenance, showering and voiding, he hit the gym for a full cardio aerobic workout followed by strength-training repetitions. He was wide awake now, feeling good and poised for action. He jumped into an orange and white spacesuit and pulled on his high-tech, high-sensitivity gloves with microencapsulated phase-change material. The gloves heightened the sensitivity of his hands and fingers, making them even more nimble and quick.

"Ten minutes to enter the Mars atmosphere."

"I hear you, FEMMIE. Just wanted one more freeze-dried burger ball before we fly the path!"

Within minutes, Derek was strapped into the pilot's seat. All systems go. He could see the meteor shower that he would be entering shortly and braced for engagement.

FEM began calling out locations and speeds of asteroids, fireballs, and shooting stars. Derek lurched the ship right, then left, then up in a ninety-degree vertical climb. A loud screech erupted as an asteroid rock scraped along the underbelly of the vessel. He straightened it out briefly until taking a deep dive and then swerved to the left to round the western side of the Red Planet. Equipped with a solar sail, he was traveling forty-percent the speed of light.

FEM's smoky, sultry voice broke into the internal, deafening white noise. *"Exceeding maximum capacity. Sail compromised by micro meteorites. Speed must be reduced or system will enforce automatic shutdown."*

"What the fuck! We never had this in the simulations!"

"I don't understand."

"No, you wouldn't!" Derek rounded the backside of Mars. It was dark, completely black and free of meteors. The sail slowly relaxed and opened to full capacity, critical for landing. He could see the lighted, glass- and metal-covered hexagonal farm below, busy with robots packaging food as they had been re-programmed to do from the NASA scientists on Earth. He eased the ship into the docking station, the solar sail billowing behind him, and latched onto the landing gear. The sail automatically flattened, then began folding up from the sides toward the center, turning it into a thin, narrow, rectangular shape. It spontaneously snapped into the open, empty SS compartment in the back of the ship.

Derek crawled out of the plane, down the tunnel into the farm, and was greeted by the managing robot. The robots had been able to accelerate the packaging of the food and preparation of the livestock to enable a seventy-two-hour turnaround. They immediately began filling the empty cargo vessel attached to the back of his ship. Derek ate and fell into a deep sleep in his bunker.

He was awakened forty-eight hours later and informed that the ship was filled and ready for takeoff. He kissed the commitment ring on his left finger, a gift from Samantha. Derek quickly boarded the jet for the return journey to Earth.

Using forward speed to achieve an aerodynamic lift from Mars, the ship rose rapidly into space. Suddenly, the aircraft was caught in an unexpected intense meteor storm that blew the ship and adjacent meteors back onto the surface of Mars. Derek quickly gained control, lightly side-swiping the hexagonal glass and metal bubble encasing the farm as he righted the craft. He reoriented the solar sail, engaged the thrusters, and soared back into space. As the jet ascended to flight path altitude, Derek watched from the cockpit windows as the farming robots–along with the cows, pigs, and chickens–were tossed about, all spinning in a concentric circles. Then debris began hitting the hull of his ship.

He swung out wider, dipping the right side down to look at the Mars farm. It was gone. The protective bubble had completely torn away and all of its contents were now joining the expanding pool of space trash.

Through a gravity-assisted trajectory, Derek deftly slingshot the aircraft further out into space. Once he was satisfied the ship was stabilized, Derek confirmed destination Earth and placed the vessel on autopilot. He strolled into the middle of the ship, which housed the sleep station. The lid of his stasis chamber was wide open. Derek stepped onto the pod's footboard, sliding his exhausted body upon the mat. Sensing the entry, the clear, impenetrable clamshell closed and locked itself in place.

"Good night, Derek. Sleep tight."

He issued FEM a thumbs-up and then pushed the internal button to activate the trans-nasal tubes. A blast of cold air blew through the miniscule nozzles embedded in the sides, quickly lowering the temperature of the chamber. Derek scanned the multimodal digital screen, verifying that his vital signs were being read and displayed. He then confirmed the calculation and timing of his hibernation termination to ensure his wakefulness upon entering Earth's atmosphere.

As his body succumbed to therapeutic hypothermia, visions of the spinning farm animals crept into Derek's mind. The only remaining, living livestock, edible food, and uncontaminated water were aboard his ship, adding grave importance to a mission already rated the highest level: Imperative.

Derek vowed to persevere and return his critical cargo safely to Earth. With his eyes closed, he imagined holding Samantha in his arms. His handsome face bore a loving smile which could easily be seen through the clear exterior walls of his hibernation chamber. Within minutes, Derek drifted into short-term cryogenic sleep.

"Twenty-four hours to enter Earth's atmosphere. Countdown begins."

Locks immediately unlatched, releasing the clamshell hatch which quickly swung wide open.

"Good morning, Derek. It's nice to have company."

Derek rubbed his eyes, slowly regaining consciousness as he remained prone in the pod. He then performed the exact same steps as before. This time, he felt really pumped up and positive. He added thirty rapid squats, fifty push-ups, and one-hundred steps to his exercise routine. The aerobic activity accelerated the flow of oxygen through his body and blood into his organs. He was prepared and ready for action.

The spacecraft powered up. Lights snapped on section by section until the entire interior was ablaze. Instrument boards lining the walls lit up and began humming, beeping, and buzzing as they performed their internal checks.

"Thirty minutes to reach Earth's atmosphere. Are you ready, Derek?"

"Of course, I am, FEMMIE! Let's go home!"

Derek strode down the hallway, grabbed a bunch of dried protein balls from the food dispenser, and gulped them down, followed by a few swigs of water from the straw-like hose attached to his flight suit's collar. He eased into the pilot seat, snapping on his chest belt. Reviewing the ship's location and scrutinizing the coordinates set to enter Earth's atmosphere, Derek instinctively knew something was wrong. The ship wouldn't enter the atmosphere at the preprogrammed coordinates. The aircraft would fly by the side of Earth, unable to establish an orbit around the planet.

Derek stared at the screen. The ship's flight path had been programmed using longitude and latitude settings that were off by nearly a quarter of an arc second–just enough to miss the entry point.

If he overrode the program, Derek would have no support from any of the other systems. He'd literally be flying solo. If the error in the calculation could be identified, he could update the input, fly the spaceship, and still depend on the auxiliary systems for assistance.

Derek tried to remember his astronomy classes to determine the cause of the discrepancy. He recalled the ecliptic coordinate system, a celestial coordinate system that represented the apparent positions and orbits of planets and solar bodies. The system's origin could be the center of the sun or Earth. He closed his eyes. It was all coming back.

The perturbing forces upon the Earth induced a slow, continuous turning of the coordinate system. The slow motion and small oscillation of the Earth's axis and the position of the vernal (northward) point on the sphere caused the ecliptic coordinate system to change accordingly. He recalled that when determining the coordinates for a planet, the equation must specify what time the vernal point and celestial equator are taken, the equinox of date. He suddenly recognized the problem. The team of physicists who programmed the spaceship had neglected to include the equinox in the equation!

Derek carefully reviewed the ecliptic longitude, latitude, and distance. He recalculated them, including the date of the equinox. Then he pulled up the data input screen, punched in the code to override the current settings, and keyed in the revised measurements. Within minutes, the final coordinates were revised and the spaceship's course corrected. The craft was now straight on a path to initiate an orbit around Earth. Upon entering the elliptical orbit, Derek would take over the controls to establish a free-return trajectory beginning the fall back to Earth.

"Two minutes to enter Earth's atmosphere."

Derek could feel the gravitational pull coming from his home planet. The sphere was growing larger in the window.

FEM spoke in her honeyed voice. *"We are inside the stratosphere. Orbital dynamics commencing."*

"I'm gonna miss working with you!"

"Likewise. I have admired your bravery and dexterity."

"Thanks, FEMMIE. Couldn't have done it without you!"

The ship shuttered, vibrated, and wobbled. Metal whined and groaned from the strength of the gravitational pull. Within moments, it stabilized itself. Derek turned off the auto-pilot and grabbed the controls. He forced the ship out of the orbital path and into a violent tail-spin trajectory speeding toward Earth. The solar sail released, slowing the spins. The cargo capsule, which was typically detached upon entry to reduce weight, had to be maintained at all costs.

Layers of the aircraft's protective, ablative covering peeled off as it hurtled through the Earth's atmosphere. Derek was aware of the flames licking at his cockpit window. With his eyes fixed to the screen, his fingers began pushing a variety of buttons in rapid succession while his forearms guided the steering sticks, relieving the pitch and roll and keeping the spaceship on course.

Static crackled loudly over the ship's speaker as FEM calmly stated, *"Two minutes to landing."*

Derek grabbed the sticks, pulling them back with all of his strength. He opened the sail to full capacity. Dark, blue-green water appeared to rise up and greet the spaceship. The craft plunged deep into the ocean, displacing a huge volume of water that created a massive plume that rose into the sky then fell with a loud splash. The jet hurtled toward the ocean's floor. The pilot swiftly engaged the thrusters and cranked on the propellers, forcing the vessel to slow, then turn, and slowly glide up to the sea's surface. Derek could hear the animals bellowing, oinking, and clucking behind him. He smiled. They were alive.

When he resurfaced, a navy aircraft carrier chugged toward him with a sizeable barge in tow. Derek popped open the hatch and poked his head out.

The navy captain spoke into a megaphone. "Derek Fentz, are you hurt?"

"No! But I sure am hungry!" All the sailors on deck burst into laughter.

"I think we can help with that!" The captain was smiling broadly. He admired this young man.

A small motorized dingy pulled up beside Derek so he could jump aboard. The barge was carefully positioned beside the cargo vessel to unload its priceless contents.

Following his space mission, Derek was isolated in confinement for a three-week period to ensure there was no presence of infection or contagion. Physicians conducted a comprehensive physical examination as well as medical, psychological, and cognitive testing. They all hoped that Derek's health and well-being had not been affected by his journey to Mars.

The exam results were normal, generally unremarkable, except for two variables: his height and his hair. Between departing from and returning to Earth, Derek had grown two inches taller. Except for the mousy, brown crop on the top of his head, he was hairless. The hair follicles on the rest of his body had been destroyed.

Typical of his engaging personality, he took the news in stride, bragging about how much taller he was than his little six-foot-one brother and never needing to shave again.

In mid-April 2042, the government released detailed information regarding the success of Derek's covert mission. On April 20, *The Washington Post* ran an article on the first page of its website:

WASHINGTON, DC–On March 20, Derek Fentz, aka video gamer "GunMic," landed safely in the Atlantic Ocean off the coast of North Carolina following the successful completion of a covert mission to Mars.

Fentz returned with viable food sources, healthy livestock, and uncontaminated water to ensure the survival of the human race. NASA has announced that the food and farm animals from the Red Planet have been relocated to an airtight, undisclosed location. Drones will soon begin distributing food allotments across the remaining five continents.

The non-GMO produce will be duplicated and grown to continue to feed the inhabitants of Earth. Fentz has been awarded the Presidential Medal of Freedom, the highest honor that can be bestowed on a US citizen. President Jones will officially present the award this evening at a black-tie event to be held at the White House.

Fentz will be joined by his fiancé, Samantha Parsons, whom Fentz claimed was the main reason he agreed to undertake the Mars mission. Dignitaries from around the world will be attending the affair to honor Fentz for his bravery, thank him for his service, and recognize his significant accomplishment of saving the human race.

<u>PYSANKY SPRING</u>

AUTHOR'S NOTE

The story "Pysanky Spring" began with the centerpiece of hand-painted wooden Russian eggs that graces our dining table each Easter. The idea of Russian Easter traditions led me to the female protagonist Babushka who speaks in broken English and Russian Proverbs. Through her, I explore Pysanky egg symbolism, Russian cuisine, and the survivor mindset. To me, Spring also represents birth, renewal of life, and growth. Those themes are presented through the second character, John. I used internal dialogue to explore John's psychology and thought process since much of his conflict and evolution is mental. I avoided an omniscient narrator so that the characters are presented to each other and to the readers simultaneously.

TJL

PYSANKY SPRING

TJ Lewes

IT HAD TAKEN NEARLY forty-five minutes to hike to the clearing, but seeing the old oak ahead energized him. He'd loved playing on that tree in his youth. *Almost there.* At the base of the tree, he dropped his duffle bag and rifled through it until finding the length of rope and the nearly empty bottle of vodka. *Just a little more.* He gulped the last of it, then sat down heavily. *You can do this.* With the empty bottle clenched between his thighs, he looped the rope around the neck to make a knot, but his left hand was clumsy and the end fell away untied. *Keep it together, man.*

He tried again, this time sliding the rope under itself and grasping it with the awkward claw on his right arm, but when he pulled, the rope slid through the metal instead of tightening upon itself. He grunted. *Nice and easy.* He grasped the rope end with his left hand and pulled, but it slid off the bottle in his legs and escaped the neck. A vein in his forehead began to bulge. *Eyes on the prize.*

On his third try, the man succeeded in tightening the rope enough to attempt throwing the bottle over the limb. *Just a little more.* The bottle arced up and over but fell short of its target. His temporal vein began to throb visibly. *Try again.* He threw the bottle harder, crashing it into the limb. It fell to the ground in front of him. He stomped as his breath steamed around him in the bitter late-March Vermont air. *Keep the end in mind.*

The fourth try resulted in the noose looped over the limb. *One step closer.* It took several more attempts for the man to repeat the feat so he could stabilize and tie off the rope. He was panting and dizzy by the time he had finished, and he laid on the ground a moment. *Good thing you bought the pre-tied noose . . . now get to it.*

On unsteady feet and with numb fingers, the man pulled a collapsible ladder from his duffle bag. It was one of the few possessions remaining from his marriage. *Don't think about her.* He focused his attention on erecting the glorified stepstool, struggling to click the pieces into their locked position. *It's going to be okay.* Before he finished, a weathered old woman in a fur coat and floral headscarf crunched into the clearing. She looked at him, the duffle bag, the bottle, the ladder, and the noose tied to the limb above. A small smile played on her lips as her heavily Russian-accented words punctuated the morning breeze.

"Zdravstvuyte comrade. Your vodka empty. Sad!"

"We are not comrades, and my vodka is not your concern."

"Ah, we enemies. Khorosho, enemies easy, friends take work. But, that tree no good. Pick different one."

"Oh, just go away and leave me alone, you crazy commie!"

Spittle flew from the man's mouth as he yelled and his face turned a dark shade of crimson. He looked ready to kill, but the little old lady just laughed at him and continued slowly down the mountain path toward the town below, an empty pack on her back. He watched her disappear into the trees. *Time to focus, man.*

Angry and frustrated, he struggled to finish assembling the ladder. His hook often caused more trouble than help, but his left hand was still not competent. *Get to it, get through it.* At last his ladder was ready and he climbed it without delay, slipping his head through the waiting noose. *Time to say goodbye.* He rocked himself forward, kicking the ladder behind him, and crashed to the ground with a heavy limb on top of him. Blackness followed.

Consciousness arrived in waves. First came pain—an agony in his side that waxed and waned with his shallow breaths. *Am I dead? Is this eternal torment?* Sound followed—the far-away rhythm of a ticking clock, the distant din of pots and pans, and nearby, the crackle of a fire. *Is there a kitchen in Hell?* Smell arrived on smoke, carrying with it the lemon-scent of clean floors and a faint aroma of roasted chicken. *Maybe my punishment is to smell food but never taste it.* Touch came slowly as his fingers twitched against soft fur above and coarse cotton below. *This feels like mink or rabbit.*

After several minutes he opened his eyes, but even with all his senses intact, he was still shocked by his surroundings. He gazed at the fireplace–a massive stone structure standing in the very center of the building; square, with an opening on each side. It spanned two stories high, decorated floor to ceiling with a hodgepodge of brightly colored tapestries, hanging baskets of decorated wooden eggs, gold-framed paintings, ceramic plates, and antlers.

He looked through the fireplace to the kitchen on the other side. White cabinets, with white walls, white countertops, and white appliances stared back at him, in stark contrast to his vibrant surroundings. Overhead, a vaulted ceiling climbed to a balcony and rooms in the back of the second floor. He followed the railing with his eyes to a staircase on the left, flanked by even more vibrant artwork and the heads of several deer and moose, and a bear.

A movement at the foot of the bed drew his gaze from the dead animals on the wall to a very alive Siberian husky laying at his feet. Its icy blue eyes seemed to bore into his soul. He raised his claw in reflex, eliciting a growl like thunder from the defensive dog.

"Natasha, niet. Idi syuda."

The dog immediately jumped from the daybed and padded over to her mistress seated in a rocking chair on the far-right side of the hearth. With head still wrapped in a floral scarf and a multicolor dress covered by a paisley shawl, the woman blended into her brummagem background. The man frowned and grumbled his disgust.

"What the hell is going on? I told you to leave me alone. Why couldn't you just let me die out there?"

"I tell you bad tree, you no listen. Bad for you. You land, I leave you alone, but this my land. You die, police come. Bad for me. I bring you here. Natasha help."

"Who are you, anyway?"

"Svetlana Ivanova Fekhlacheva."

"I asked you for your name, not to be sworn at, you batty Bolshevik. I'm outta here."

The man attempted to stand, but a searing pain tore through his body, dropping him back onto the daybed. He panted from the agonizing jolt as sweat broke out on his forehead. He tried to wipe it with his right hand, jabbing himself with his claw. He crossed his arms in front of him and stared straight up at the ceiling, determined to not speak to that maddening woman again. Several minutes passed before she stood to leave, whispering only three words before heading to the kitchen.

"Call me Babushka."

He watched her through the fireplace. As the flames danced, the old woman seemed to move with them and in them. From his perspective, the old woman was flame from the waist down and body from the belt up. It seemed dark and evil. *Just my luck, I'm alive but in Hell anyway. I'll spend eternity arguing with some ancient immigrant, locked inside a Russian kaleidoscope, guarded by a one-headed Cerberus named Natasha.*

Before he could think further, Babushka shuffled into the room with a tray table, cutlery, and a steaming plate. He didn't want to admit it, but the aroma wafting in his direction was the finest he had smelled in nearly a year. The woman quickly set up the table and plate, before turning her attention to him. She extended a hand.

"You sit now, John."

Before he could even form a retort, she slid him into a seated position, turning his legs and propping his back on a pillow. The pain made him cry out, but she didn't acknowledge it. She turned to leave, when the man suddenly realized she had called him by name.

"Wait, how did you know my name?"

"I find papers in bag."

Babushka said nothing more and retired to the kitchen. John thought about the papers within his duffle bag: Driver's license. Termination notice. Foreclosure documents and repo letter. Letter to his ex-wife. Journal. Will. *She knows every goddamn thing about me! That's an intrusion of privacy.*

The food called John's attention before he could voice his complaint. Somewhere between the crispy skin of his roasted chicken and the buttery chunks in his mashed potatoes, John forgot about everything. While he ate, his mind was silent and his body reveled in the simple pleasure of food and warmth. He laid back on the pillow completely satiated and slept soundly until morning.

He awoke to a plate of fried eggs with kielbasa and dill. The bread beside it was black but wasn't pumpernickel. A lukewarm cup of tea, with a slice of lemon on one side and a small glass sugar dish on the other, completed the tray table buffet. He sat up painfully, looking for Babushka, but could not see her anywhere from his perch. John tore into his breakfast. It was the first time in many months that he had eaten two hot meals consecutively.

A pressing need forced John to abandon his meal halfway through. He rose to his feet painfully and shuffled through the house in search of a bathroom. He found neither bathroom nor Babushka on the main floor. In agony from his broken ribs, John ascended the stairs and found the restroom behind the first door off the balcony.

While he washed his hand, through the window he saw the old woman climbing the path home. John descended the stairs and crossed to the doorway, where he found his duffle bag on the floor. He dug through it to find that the ladder and rope were gone. By the time Babushka entered, her pack laden with goods, John was sweating and shaking. She eyed him carefully.

"Dobroye utro, John"

"Yeah, Doberman uterus right back atcha. Listen, I'm leaving."

"You leave? Hmmmm . . . where you go? Different tree?"

John's eyes went cold and his fist clenched. The truth was, he had nowhere to go. His dad was in jail, and his mom had disappeared years ago. He had no known family, and now lacked the supplies he needed to complete his mission. Beyond that, just the trip to the bathroom had depleted him, and John knew he could not make the hike back to town or even lift his nearly empty duffle bag. He spoke through gritted teeth.

"That's not your business, Babushka."

"True, but you owe me. In Russia we say: Gólod ne tyótka. Birds no fly into mouth roasted. You take two meals and one-night bed. You pay, then you go."

"What are you talking about? You really are crazy. You saw my papers. I don't have a single cent to my name. How the hell am I supposed to pay you?"

"Easy. You work."

"Look at me Babushka . . . I'm missing an arm. I can't do anything. I can't work. I'm useless!"

Babushka stared silently at John for a long time, letting his final words hang in the room. His face was red, his hand was trembling, and tears threatened to spill from his angry eyes. She spoke firmly.

"Comrade, value of man not hand, but head and heart. Now, you wash dishes."

Babushka retrieved her heavy pack and went to the kitchen. She put away her purchases then retired to a small craft table in the corner where she kept her paints and wooden eggs. She settled in, her back to the kitchen, and began working on a new design she had envisioned on her hike to the store that morning. She bent her head and focused on her pysanka, blocking out her surroundings completely.

It took Babushka nearly three hours to complete the intricate design on her wooden egg. Lengthwise she began with two purple eternity bands, crossing on the top and bottom, to represent infinity and immortality. In one quadrant she painted a green ladder to symbolize prosperity and growth. In the next, an orange sun for fortune and enlightenment. She adorned the third quadrant with a red bird for fulfillment of desires. The last section she painted her wishes for health in yellow wheat.

Babushka walked into the kitchen to prepare lunch and was pleasantly surprised to see the dishes drying next to the sink. The water on the floor and the ripped washcloth attested to an epic battle. Smiling, she cleaned up the spill and prepared a beef and buckwheat soup along with an Olivier salad. She set lunch out on the dining table, then went to find John. He was lying on the daybed, eyes open but unfocused, tears streaming down his cheeks unnoticed.

"Come comrade, eat."

John jerked at her voice, moaning in pain, but rose to follow her to the dining table without complaint. They ate in silence. Babushka looked around the room with misty eyes as she picked at her food. John noticed the highly polished furniture and glass were pristine and the throw rug below was free of footprints, except for the ones they just made.

"You don't eat in here much, do ya? This room looks like a museum, completely untouched."

"No eat here since husband die."

"I'm sorry. When did he pass?"

"Easter 2003."

"Don't your kids or friends visit and eat here sometimes, or maybe a boyfriend?"

"No kids. No friends. No boyfriend."

Babushka spit the last word as she huffed from the dining room. She passed by a moment later with her coat and her dog, then trudged out the front door. John remained inside, considering what she had said. *For the last fifteen years, Babushka has survived on her own, and I haven't lasted ten months. What magical quality does she have that I don't?*

John pondered that question as he cleared the table, stored the leftovers, and washed the dishes. Then he went to the daybed to nap, exhausted and confused.

Babushka was rattling in the kitchen when he awoke after sunset. John watched her through the fireplace, as she industriously chopped vegetables, her face showing no sign of her previous anguish. He shuffled to the kitchen to help, calling from the doorway to not startle her.

"Hi, Babushka. Are you okay? Listen, sorry about earlier. We don't need to eat in the dining room."

She looked at him, surprised not by his voice but by his words. Babushka laughed and then shook her head.

"Volkóv boyát'sa—v les ne khodít. Fear wolves, never go to woods? Pshaw."

"But Babushka, it clearly hurt you. Why do it again?"

"Because grief like ocean. It come in waves. Some waves knock you down. Stand up again. Next wave not so big. Ocean beautiful because heart swim there. Here. Put this on dining table."

Babushka handed him a large plate of smoked salmon and crème fraiche crepes, then turned to the counter to gather the plates, silverware, and bowls of borscht. John stood in place thinking about what she had said. *Grief hits you in waves. If you get knocked down, you gotta stand back up. You gotta face the ocean if you want to touch your heart.* It resonated.

Babushka strode past him and settled herself at the dining table. John joined her, setting the laden plate down with a clumsy thud. He sat down, head bent, embarrassed by his perpetual ineptitude.

"Kon' o chetyryókh nogakh, da i tot spotykáetsya. Horse has four good legs, still stumbles."

John jerked his head up at her comment. *Can she read my mind?* He stared at the old woman slurping borscht and considered her words. *A horse has four good legs, but still stumbles. I guess she means to err is human. Four good legs huh, I bet she wonders how I lost my hand. Should I tell her? Can I handle the wave? Maybe that's what she meant by not being afraid to go into the woods just because you fear the wolves.* John swallowed deeply, his hand clenched under the table.

"I lost my hand in a work accident in construction. We were in a

125

remote location removing boulders from a build site. The cable lifting the load broke, and my right hand was crushed. It took hours for them to get a replacement cable to lift the boulder off me. It was too late for my hand, so they amputated and gave me this ridiculous contraption."

John flourished his hook and awaited the old woman's next Russian proverb. She didn't speak. Instead she reached her hands across the table, grasping his hand in one and his claw in the other. She looked at him sympathetically and nodded her head in understanding. Instead of the expected wave of grief, John felt unburdened. Just sharing his grief had lightened its load. He decided to continue his tale.

"After the accident, I was unable to work. Six months later, my employer dropped me. A few months after that, my wife left me. I lost my house and car. I have nothing left, Babushka. Where do I go from here?"

She didn't answer, but instead slipped from the room. Babushka returned a moment later with a bottle of Tovaritch vodka and two glasses. She did not bring ice or juice. She sat the bottle in front of John, then looked him in the eyes.

"In vodka, you start top and work to bottom. In life, you start bottom and work to top."

She deftly opened the bottle and poured two glasses. She held hers to her nose, inhaling the heady fumes with her eyes closed. John took his glass and followed suit. It smelled nothing like the Smirnoff he had guzzled two nights ago. *Was it only two nights ago that I packed my duffle bag and wrote my will and letter to my ex? Was it only yesterday that I tried to end my life?* The glass in his hand reverberated as Babushka clanked cups.

"Za zdaróvye comrade."

"To you, Babushka."

Together they took a deep gulp from their glasses, both exhaling at the same time. Babushka giggled, and John felt a smile force itself onto his face. He looked at his hostess carefully. Her eyes sparkled and her crow's feet danced above high cheekbones. John wondered what motivated his new companion.

"Babushka, if you won the lottery, what would you do with the money?"

"Hmmmm. Big money? I fix barn, buy plane ticket for sister in

Russia, and hire taxi to get groceries. Maybe buy new snow boots. You?"

"First, I'd buy a decent prosthetic–the ones that work like real hands. Then, I think I'd buy a piece of land and build a log cabin. I'd get myself a jeep and a pool. I think I'd like to try carving again, too. I was really good before, and maybe I could try again."

John's voice tapered off as he considered it. He and Babushka finished their glasses in silence, then cleared the table together. In the kitchen, they both washed and dried the dishes, then packed away the leftovers. Babushka sang softly to herself as she worked. John was haunted by the tune.

"What song is that Babushka?"

"'Katyusha.' About girl who love soldier. He far away. She wait patient. We all must."

With that, Babushka retired upstairs to bed and John reclined on the daybed. His body was exhausted, but his mind was more awake than it had been in months. *Imagine how great it would be, that cabin with a pool. I could have a workshop and carve again. It would take a lot of practice, and patience, and work, but maybe it's possible. In vodka you start from the top and work down, in life you start from the bottom and work up. I guess sometimes, you gotta open a new bottle and a new life and start the process over.*

John awoke to a tray table breakfast. His joy from the prior night was replaced by pain in his sides, but he could get around the house without much trouble. Like every morning, Babushka was already up and out. Curious, John decided to venture outside.

The gravel driveway in front of the house was overgrown and looked like it hadn't been used in many years. It stretched beyond view, and John wondered what road it connected to. Far to the right, John saw a dilapidated barn. He walked to it slowly, surprised to hear animals within.

Inside he found a cow, two goats, and several chickens. The roof above had been patched with tapestries and scarves. Some areas were completely open. The walls had several missing slats, and the loft was no longer serviceable. Despite its ramshackle structure, the barn was swept clean, and the animals each had secure stalls with fresh food and new water.

John wandered behind the house and found a flower garden erupting in early spring buds. Forsythia, tulips, crocus, daffodils, violets, and primrose spilled out of untended beds. The brick-lined pathways were covered in old leaves and weeds. John was surprised. *The house and barn are meticulously attended, why is the garden such a mess?*

As he scanned the garden again, John noticed a garage nestled between trees on the far side of the house. He picked his way over to the structure, but his ribs shrieked in protest when he attempted to lift the garage door. The door to the right was unlocked, so he let himself in. The first thing John noticed was a late-90s Ford pickup truck. It was coated in dust, and one of the tires was flat, but he saw no signs of corrosion.

John looked around the rest of the garage. One side was filled with building materials—two-by-fours, shingles, siding. The entire top half of the back wall was fitted with hooks displaying a bevy of tools. Below, a workbench presented a table saw and various unfinished projects. Ladders, shovels, rakes, and a hoe leaned against the near wall next to piles of netting, tarp, and rope. John inhaled sharply as his eyes scanned back over the contents of the garage. *Everything I need to complete my mission is right here in this room.*

He wedged the necessary materials under his hooked stump and dragged the large ladder from the garage to the barn. *The loft should work.* Although he was in pain, he worked as fast as he could. *Gotta get done before Babushka returns.*

Babushka walked slowly. She usually made the journey to town twice a week. She had done so three times in three days because of her houseguest, and her body protested every step. Up the path and to the left, her garage peaked out of early spring foliage. When she noticed the open door, her heart began to race. She dropped her bag on the trail and dashed toward the garage. John was not there, but she noticed the missing ladder.

She checked the house but found nothing. Through the window she noticed the open barn door. Babushka's heart dropped to her stomach, then flip-flopped back to her chest. She took a deep breath, then walked to the barn with heavy steps. Although she braced herself for the worst, she was not prepared for what she saw.

John was sitting in the corner with a goat cuddling on either side of him, laughing. The roof above was partially patched, and half of the missing wall slats had been replaced by siding. John looked up at Babushka, his eyes shining with the exhilaration of accomplishment.

"Welcome home, Babushka! I wanted to have it done before you got back, but it took a long time. I'll finish before sundown tomorrow. It's not perfect, but I did it!"

"Pérvyy blin vsegdá kómom. First pancake always blob. Spasíbo, John. Come, eat, then work more."

She retrieved her pack from the path before reporting to the kitchen. Her body didn't hurt anymore and suddenly she felt inspired.

While eating a late lunch with John, she thought about how to show her appreciation for his work on the barn. Easter was two days away, and Babushka wanted to make it one neither of them would forget. She considered her menu carefully and decided that it was time to return to her roots.

She would make Paskha, a cheese dessert with eggs, butter, raisins, and almonds. They would dine on lamb, potatoes, and peas, with Kulich bread and red hard-boiled eggs, just as she had done in her youth and with her husband every year before he died. It meant another trip to town in the morning, and an inevitable trip down memory lane the following day, but she would not be deterred.

She left at the first rays of light, and John began working on the barn shortly after. When she returned, Babushka prepared the Paskha to cool by morning, and the Kulich dough to rise by night. She also dyed the eggs and worked on her special surprise. John hammered away in the barn, securing the last shingle as the sun began to dip behind the mountain. From his rooftop perch he watched it set. *It's not just ending a day, but an era.*

That night Babushka and John dined on leftovers, washed down with vodka. Afterward, Babushka disappeared for a few minutes upstairs. She returned with a pair of men's pajamas, some new underwear and socks, a running suit, and a bag of toiletries. She also carried a pair of khakis and a cashmere sweater. They still had tags but smelled like mothballs. She laid them on the table in front of John and patted his hand.

"Take shower John, then rest. Tomorrow use good clothes. At sunrise we pray, then we eat."

John did as instructed, enjoying every drop of hot shower water on his fatigued muscles. Although his ribs were still bruised and sore, John no longer suffered the pain of self-pity. In rebuilding the barn, he had begun to rebuild himself. The shingles were crooked, and the siding wasn't straight, but the structure was sound. *That barn's a lot like me.*

Early the next morning, an hour before sunrise, Babushka woke John. In the pre-dawn darkness, they hiked up the mountain, to a small clearing on the summit. Although the hills usually echoed with a symphony of birds and bugs, not a sound was heard. They dared not disturb the silence. Slowly, the sky around them transitioned from gray to a blazing pink and purple, the clouds above them reflecting shades of cyan. John was transfixed.

As the sun finally crested the hills to the east, Babushka began a Russian Liturgy. John didn't understand a word she said, but somehow it didn't matter. He could feel the light enter his body and push out the darkness. When the sun had completely risen, Babushka stopped her sermon and said simply: "He risen."

She clapped John on the shoulder, a wide smile on her face as she turned to leave. John remained in the clearing a moment longer in thought. *He is risen. I don't think she was talking only about Jesus.* He smiled and followed the old lady home, struggling to keep up with her. Once at the house, instead of taking him inside, she led him to her flower garden. She skipped the last few steps over to a basket and clasped her hands in excitement.

"I make you Easter egg hunt. In garden, I hide twenty-four pysanky, special eggs for you. You find, you win prize. Much fun. I cook."

Babushka patted his back, pushing him toward the garden as she retired to the house. John saw her face appear in the kitchen window. She waved at him, and he set to work. It took him several minutes to find the first egg. It was deep inside a forsythia bush, hidden completely from view until he laid on the ground. *She's not making this easy for me . . . good.*

Over the next two hours, John found twenty-three eggs. His ribs ached from climbing through the overgrowth and crawling under plants, but he was enjoying himself completely. He pushed aside some primrose leaves and discovered a small wooden box half-buried in the soil. It was chipped and weathered, but he could hear something inside. He couldn't find a way to open it, so he put it in his basket and continued with the hunt.

John was halfway through the tulips when he finally found the last egg. It looked different than the others. Instead of a symmetric design, it had four quadrants painted with symbols, each different than the next. John carried the basket over his right arm but held the special egg and the strange box in his left hand. He found the dining table laid out in blue and white porcelain dishes and crystal glassware. John set the basket by his chair, slipped the box and unique pysanka into his coat pockets, washed his hand, then helped Babushka carry their feast to the table, his belly growling loudly. She laughed out loud.

"You find all pysanky, da? We check after dinner. Eat comrade. I cut Kulich last."

She pointed to the tall loaf of bread in the center of the table, surrounded by red-dyed eggs and a selection of meats and cheeses. A rack of lamb with potatoes and peas beckoned John first. The meat was juicy and fell from the bone. He cleared his plate, then ate a cold red egg from the serving plate in front of him. Babushka watched him a moment, before pointing at the dyed egg.

"Red color, life and victory. Today good day for Christians and you. Here, Paskha. Kulich. You like. Try."

John looked at the cold mass of curded farmer's cheese she called Paskha. It resembled frozen cottage cheese, almost like chunky ice cream. John tasted it hesitantly. He picked up the flavors of almond, lemon, orange, and vanilla mixed into the delicious curds. He nodded as he chewed, quick to take another bite as Babushka sliced her Easter bread and handed him a piece.

"Here, put Paskha on Kulich."

John took a bite of the cheese-covered bread. It was a cross between brioche and cake, crumbly but dense and a little sweet. Inside were raisins, nuts, and candied citrus rinds. A quiet moan of contentment escaped him, much to Babushka's delight. They finished dessert, sipped coffee and cleared the table, then returned to the dining room for the Easter basket.

"Look Babushka, I found all the eggs. Count them!"

She grinned, remembering how excited her husband had always been to play their little game. They did an egg hunt every year since marriage, first to practice for future children, then to embody the children they would never have. Her husband had died during their annual Easter egg hunt from a massive heart attack, but fifteen years later she remembered the joy it had always brought them. She closed her eyes for a moment to stop the flow of tears, then proceeded to count the eggs.

"Twenty-three. Tsk-tsk, John."

He withdrew the last egg from his pocket, setting it proudly with the others. Each one was a work of art, some geometric, some floral, some a cacophony of birds and vinery. Each one was unique, but all of them beautiful. Each was symmetric except the last, making it seem extra special to him.

"Babushka, why is this egg different? What does it mean?"

"Purple circles, infinity and immortality. Green ladder, prosperity and growth. Orange sun, fortune and enlightenment. Red bird fill wishes. Health, yellow wheat. Special pysanka. You keep. You also take this. Good truck, need work."

She handed John the keys to the Ford. He was overwhelmed by the gesture. He stared silently at the keys for several moments.

"Thank you, Babushka." His voice was thick with emotion. "I have something for you, too. I found it buried in the garden under the primrose. I don't know what's inside."

John produced the wooden box from his pocket and presented it to Babushka. Her eyes immediately flashed recognition, but it took her hand several moments to reach out for the box. She cradled it to her chest, rocking slowing back and forth, as tears streamed down her wrinkled cheek. John stood behind her and rubbed her shoulder with his good hand, unsure what to do. She reached up and patted his hand, before clearing her throat to speak.

"Before he die, my husband hide Easter surprise for me. After he die, I no look. Too afraid of wolves and waves. Now I face. Good. Vrémya–lúchshiy dóktor. Time best healer. You check car, I check box."

John hurried to the garage, keys in hand, and Babushka remained in the dining room, still clenching the box. She ran her fingers over the intricate carvings, thinking about her husband's hands hard at work making them for her. She recognized the design of her husband's puzzle box and depressed a small carved bird on the back corner. A latch swung out, which she pushed down, opening the lid.

Within the watertight box, Babushka found a cinched velvet sack, encasing a golden, jewel-encrusted egg. The egg was finely crafted in red enamel with gold leaves that branched from a hinged opening. Eyes wide, she opened the Fabergé egg to reveal a miniature bouquet of flowers, comprised of ruby roses, diamond lilies, and sapphire delphiniums with emerald leaves in a gold vase. Her eyes filled with tears once again.

On their last Easter together, Babushka had felt sad that her husband hadn't gotten her a bouquet as he'd done during all their previous Easters together. He had been very busy travelling for business in the weeks before the holiday, and she thought he had forgotten about her. Now, she realized that he had purchased her a bouquet of the finest flowers on Earth. She whispered her love to the empty room.

"Ya lyublyu tebya."

This egg was the answer to her daily prayer. Seven years before his death, her husband had taken a thirty-year mortgage to purchase their property. After his death she had paid faithfully every month, but eight years of payments remained, and she had less than $1,000 left to her name. The morning she first met John, she had been on her way to the real estate office to list her beloved homestead for sale. In stopping to save him, she had managed to save herself. Babushka laughed aloud.

In the garage, John felt equally thrilled. The truck had an extended cab and a pristine interior with the lingering odor of a new vehicle. It didn't start when he turned the key, but he found an electric car charger in the garage and jumped the battery. The old pickup came to life reluctantly with a sputter and a growl. He knew he would have to buy a new tire, and then drive it to the nearest garage for a complete tune-up, but he delighted in the opportunities that were open to him.

Back inside, John and Babushka sat together at the table once again, half a bottle of vodka in front of them. They both had eyes filled with dreams as their bellies filled with liquor. They laughed and cried and then laughed some more. At the end of the bottle, John grasped Babushka's hand, looking serious.

"Listen Babushka, thank you so much for the truck. I promise to take you to the store anytime you want to go, just as soon as I clear the driveway so we can get to the road. I promise I will pay you back for everything have done for me."

"Driveway job, very long, very big. We own much land here, over one-hundred acres. Skóro skázka skázyvayetsya, da ne skóro délo délaetsya. Story tell fast, but work go slow. If you clear driveway, I give you some land. You pick good place. I buy supplies and you build house. Da?"

John stared at her blankly a moment as he processed her words. *If I clear her driveway, she'll give me a plot of land and all the supplies I need to build my house?* He grinned widely, swaying slightly from drink.

"No problem Babs, you're on!"

The old lady nodded knowingly, a small smile on her flushed face.

"Pey, da délo razuméy. Drink, but be expert in business. Remember comrade, Ugovór dorózhe déneg. Contract more value than money. Before we make final contract, we sleep. Útro véchera mudrenéye. Morning wiser than evening."

With that, she disappeared to the kitchen with her glass and empty vodka bottle. John didn't follow. Instead he sat at the table, thinking. *Where should I build? I can finish the driveway in a week, and after that I can have my cabin done by fall. It'll be great.*

John awoke early the next morning, still seated at the table, with a headache. He rose quickly, eager to begin. He decided to walk the driveway to the road and back, both to gauge the work needed and to begin looking for plots. He set off briskly, but soon found himself climbing over large limbs. A mile into his hike he found an entire fallen tree.

The driveway extended nearly two miles, and not a square inch of it was clear. Any place that didn't have branches was covered in leaves above with weeds sprouting from below. He sat where the driveway met the road, and was overwhelmed by the enormity of the task at hand. *A week? This will take forever. There's no way. No way.*

He began his long walk back angrily, headache worse than ever, and stomach aching from hunger. As he crunched down the driveway a second time, his mind began to see a glimmer of possibility. *The small branches are easy enough. Just pile them in the woods on either side and they'll be fine. I could cut the downed tree into smaller pieces. There's a chainsaw in the garage. Once I clear the debris from the garage to the tree, I could transport the pieces by vehicle. Maybe if I just split the tree into firewood, I could stock Babushka and myself for next winter. With the sticks out of the way, a leaf-blower should clear the rest, and maybe a weedwhacker.* Little by little, the obstacles began looking like opportunities.

He found Babushka in the kitchen, a large plate of Easter leftovers ready for him. He accepted it gratefully and led the way to the dining table, mind still reeling from his morning walk. He ate a few bites quickly, before Babushka interrupted him.

"You see whole driveway, da? Big job. Big work. You do?"

"Yes, I'll do it, but to be honest I feel a little daunted. It's a big job, and I'm scared about how to pull it off and how long it will take."

"You no worry. Glazá boyátsya, a rúki délayut. Eyes afraid, but hand do work. Relax. Terpéniye i trud vsyo peretrút. Patience and time fray through everything comrade. Today start driveway, tomorrow we get tire, and soon you build house."

It took John nearly two months to get the old Ford running and clear the driveway, but on the last day of May, the odd pair climbed into the cab for their maiden voyage. John sat a few moments in the driver's seat flexing his new prosthetic hand before backing slowly out of the garage, Babushka smiling broadly at him from the passenger seat.

He drove her to the grocery store first, then to the post office to send a plane ticket to her sister. Halfway back down the driveway home he pulled over to the side. Together John and Babushka walked to a clearing twenty yards into the woods overlooking the town far below.

"I think I found my spot, Babushka."

"I think too, John."

Her voice held a hint of humor, and he realized she meant he had found his place in more ways than just one. He nodded in understanding, his voice a chuckle.

"It's like winning the lottery."

"Da comrade, for us both."

FOR THE COMMON GOOD

AUTHOR'S NOTE

"For the Common Good" was conceived several years ago as a two-act play. I recall feeling quite pleased with the end product at that time. Shortly thereafter, a director/friend asked to read it. I was short on time and sent him the original manuscript.

A few months later, his house tragically burned to the ground, taking the play with it. I've never tried to recreate the original, but am satisfied with the short story version of the tale which appears on the following pages.

Maybe sometime in the future I'll endeavor to reconstruct the play version. The whole concept of our government taking charge of a serious epidemic both fascinates and frightens me. Hopefully, such extremes will never happen.

DWD

FOR THE COMMON GOOD

David W. Dutton

IN THE ELITE WASHINGTON, DC, suburb of Georgetown, Kevin Hopkins pulled his duffel bag from the back seat of the cab and stood staring up at the tall Georgian townhouse. It was painted white brick with severe, black shutters. He was home again. His sophomore year at MIT was behind him.

Summer vacation stretched ahead. That would mean working at his father's architectural office as he had all the summers before. His father, Gerald, was a nationally known architect who had risen to the post of National Architect for the New Regime. That was twenty years ago, in 2053, following the collapse of the democratic government under President Truman Coverdale. That had been a time of much upheaval. Coverdale been had indicted on various charges and summarily impeached. Against the terms of the old Constitution, his vice president had been rejected by Congress. Control of the government was then seized by a faction within Congress, and, since then, nothing had been the same. There were changes within every facet of life . . . some good . . . some not so good. Fortunately for Kevin, his family had been on the winning side and now reaped the benefits allotted to those in power. Gerald Hopkins was responsible for the design and construction of the six, great AIDS camps deemed necessary to protect the populace from an ever-spreading HIV-3 outbreak. This latest strain was more contagious and lethal than HIV-1 and HIV-2 combined. The country was in a panic. Kevin was well schooled in the philosophy behind the camps, but didn't necessarily believe all he was told.

Kevin hefted his duffel bag and climbed the limestone steps to the large front door. He punched in the security code, and the heavy, black door swung slowly open. The lofty foyer beyond was as cold and unforgiving as he'd remembered. The black marble floor flowed across the vast space to the curved stairway with its black and silver Regency railing. The white limestone walls glowed softly, completely devoid of any decoration or embellishment. To his left, the ebony doors to the library were closed tightly. To his right, the doors to the living room stood open, beckoning him to enter.

Kevin set his duffel bag at the foot of the stair. "Hey! I'm home!"

His shout went unanswered, swallowed in the gloom.

With a sigh, Kevin turned and headed toward the living room. He hadn't expected a welcoming party. Why was he surprised?

The living room was as unwelcoming as the foyer: thick, white carpeting, ebony furniture with white velvet upholstery, lots of crystal and silver. Beyond the black marble colonnade at the rear of the room, the vast dining room lay in shadow. He crossed it quickly, walked through the butler's pantry, and pushed open the door to the kitchen. It, too, was a study in chiaroscuro: black appliances, white cabinetry, black and white tile floor. But it was the woman peeling potatoes at the center island who caught his attention.

Rachel Wilson had been with the Hopkins family as long as Kevin could remember. Her once-auburn hair was now streaked with gray. Perhaps she moved a bit slower these days, but she still retained the tough Irish constitution that had seen her through so much. Kevin well remembered the day she had joined the ranks of the other domestics marching on the Capitol to protest the banning of dishwashers and washing machines in the name of water conservation. Gerald Hopkins had been furious, and Kevin had been afraid Rachel would be sent away. If not for his mother, Maureen, she probably would have.

Rachel looked up as Kevin entered the room. A broad smile greeted him. "Master Kevin! You're home!" She lay down her work, wiped her hands on her apron, and hurried toward him.

Slipping her arms around Kevin, she hugged him fiercely. "It be a blessing to see you."

Kevin laughed. "Can't we discard the 'Master' epithet? I am

twenty-one, you know."

Rachel ruffled his thick, black hair and kissed him lightly on the cheek before returning to her work. "Ah, ye shall always be my little lad." She smiled. "I can still see you and my Sarah running and playing in the garden."

Kevin plopped down on a bar stool across from her. "Where is everybody?"

"Ah, your mum is at some fund raiser at the Smithsonian. Your dad, of course, is at the office."

Kevin laughed. "Of course!" He fiddled with an envelope lying on the counter in front of him. It was addressed to Sarah Wilson from the State Health Coalition. "How is Sarah? Is she here?"

Rachel glanced at the digital readout on the stove. "Be about any minute now I would be thinking. She's just finishing her classes for the day."

"How's she making out with them?"

"Oh, they be hard enough, mind you, but she's doin' grand. Just don't think nursing was what she really wanted."

Kevin nodded. "Yeah . . . I don't think so either."

Rachel sighed. "Well, that's what she drew at the job symposium, so I guess we just have to believe the Labor Department knows what's best."

Kevin laughed. "If you say so." Selecting a person's future by ballot seemed a poor way to fuel the work force, but that was how it was done. Of course, that didn't apply to Kevin and his kind. They were given free rein to choose any profession that would benefit the New Regime.

Sarah was Rachel's granddaughter. When her parents were killed during a protest march, Sarah was only five years old. With no other alternative, Family Resource and Planning had given her to Rachel to raise. Rachel happily accepted the ruling, and the two of them had lived in the small apartment above the kitchen wing of the Hopkins house for the last fifteen years. Sarah and Kevin had been inseparable while growing up. Gerald Hopkins had not approved. He felt it wasn't fitting that the two of them play together, but Maureen had won that battle. Now that they were older, their relationship had blossomed into something beyond friendship–a secret known only to Rachel. Kevin's parents, particularly Gerald, could not be entrusted with that information.

Sarah Wilson burst into the room. Her thick, auburn hair was pulled back and secured at the nape of her neck. She dropped her tote bag and ran toward Kevin. "You're home!" She threw her arms around him.

Kevin smiled. "Yep. You've got to put up with me for the next three months."

Sarah leaned back, stared at him, and then kissed him firmly on the lips.

"Hey, hey! There'll be none of that in my kitchen. You can't be acting like that in public."

Sarah broke the kiss and smiled. "Oh, Gram, your kitchen is hardly a public place."

"You never know when the Mister or the Missus might be a'coming through that door. It's getting on to their time, you know."

Sarah sat on the stool next to Kevin and held both of his hands in hers. "God, you look good!"

"I might say the same for you."

"That missive came for you today." Rachel indicated the letter lying on the counter.

Sarah glanced at the envelope. "Probably just a follow-up from when I was in the clinic."

Eighteen months earlier, Sarah had been struck by a car on her way to class. Her injuries were severe, and she had spent over a month at the Public Clinic. Kevin was at school at the time. When he heard about the accident, he had phoned his father and pleaded with him to have Sarah moved to a private facility. Gerald refused, explaining that favors within the Regime were only to be used in cases of dire emergency. Sarah, he'd affirmed, would receive sufficient care at the Public Clinic.

Sarah scanned the letter. "I have to report back to the clinic tomorrow morning at 8:00 AM."

Kevin looked perplexed. "Tomorrow's Saturday."

Sarah laughed. "Tell *them* that. It's probably just another formality."

"Do you want me to go with you?"

"Kevin, you know that can't happen. What would you tell your parents?"

Kevin took Sarah's hand. "Then meet me in the courtyard when you get back." He smiled. "At our secret place."

Rachel sadly shook her head.

Unlike the house, the courtyard was a riot of color. The gardeners had planted the first of the summer flowers, and everything was fresh and green. Kevin slipped through the French doors from the foyer and stood looking around to make sure he was alone. He followed the stone path around the fountain and down the far side of the courtyard. There, in a bower of yellow jasmine and red honeysuckle, was a stone bench where Sarah would be waiting.

Kevin turned the final curve in the path, ducked under a trellis, and entered their sanctuary.

Sarah was sitting on the bench. She was crying quietly.

"What's wrong?" Kevin sat beside her and wrapped his arm around her shoulders. "What happened?"

"Oh, Kevin, it's horrible!" With a sob, she lay her head against his chest.

He kissed the top of her head. "Tell me."

"The Clinic. I had to have blood work done."

"Why?"

"There was a contamination issue with the blood they used for my transfusions."

Kevin was silent for a second. "And?"

Sarah sobbed again. "I tested positive."

"Oh, my God."

"I have to report Monday morning. I'm being transferred to the AIDS camp outside of Syracuse."

Kevin squeezed her tightly. "That's . . . that's not happening. I'll talk to Dad tonight. He'll be able to do something." He kissed the top of her head again. "Don't worry. He'll take care of it."

Evening cocktails in the library were customary in the Hopkins house. The black walls and leather furniture set the tone for serious discussions. Tonight would be no different.

Kevin faced his father across the table in front of the black marble fireplace. Maureen relaxed on the adjacent sofa.

Kevin fiddled with his glass and then looked up at his father. "How are the AIDS camps coming?"

Gerald laughed. "Splendidly! Of course, you'll find out for

yourself come Monday. Still plenty of work to be done. Now that Syracuse and Atlanta are up and running, we're concentrating on San Diego and Portland."

Kevin sipped his Manhattan and nodded. "Big business."

Gerald nodded. "Sure is. Unfortunate for some, but still the best solution for the problem."

Kevin stared at his father before speaking. "You really think so?"

"Of course! The population has to be protected." Gerald took a swallow of his drink. "It's the perfect solution."

Kevin rose from his chair and stood in front of the fireplace. He sipped his drink and looked from his mother to his father. "We have a problem."

Maureen set down her glass. "What is it, dear?"

"Sarah."

Maureen looked concerned. "What's wrong with Sarah?"

Kevin drew a deep breath and took another drink. "The blood they transfused her with at the clinic was contaminated. They tested her this morning. She's positive."

Maureen gasped. "Oh, dear. That's terrible!"

Gerald downed the remainder of his brandy. "Are they sure?"

"I guess so. She's been ordered to report on Monday morning to be transferred to Syracuse."

"Gerald! You have to do something! That poor girl can't be sent to one of those camps! It's too horrible to imagine!"

Kevin looked at his father. Gerald sat staring at his empty glass. Silence filled the room.

"Dad?"

Gerald turned his empty glass between his thumb and forefinger.

Maureen sat on the edge of the sofa. "Gerald?"

"Well . . . I don't know as there's much I can do."

"Gerald, you certainly must know someone."

"It's not as simple as that."

"When I asked you to have her moved to a private hospital, you said favors could only be used in cases of dire emergencies. Well, this is a dire emergency!"

Gerald picked up the decanter and refilled his snifter. "Actually, it isn't."

Maureen looked shocked. "What do you mean? Of course it is!"

Gerald sighed and took a sip of the brandy. "Sarah isn't in our family."

Kevin glared at his father. "Of course she is! We grew up together!"

"She's not blood. We're not qualified to intercede for her."

Kevin slammed his glass down on the mantel. "That's ridiculous!"

"Perhaps . . . but that's the way it works."

Kevin paused and glanced at his mother. "But . . . but I love her. Someday, we're going to be married."

Gerald laughed. "Don't be ridiculous. She's not a qualified consort for someone in your position."

Maureen was aghast. "Gerald . . . please . . . "

Gerald looked at his wife. "I'm sorry, dear. I don't make the rules."

"Rules! Always the damn rules!" Kevin stepped away from the fireplace and headed toward the foyer. "It's always either wrong or right." He paused. "There's never any gray anymore."

He was met with silence.

The following Sunday at 3:00 PM Maureen walked into the kitchen. Rachel sat at the island and stared at the counter top, her hands folded in her lap.

"Dinner about ready? You know Mr. Hopkins likes to eat at three on Sundays."

Rachel sighed. "I'm sorry, Mum. I'm a bit behind my time today. It won't be much longer."

Maureen smiled. "That's all right. I'll fix him another cocktail." She turned to leave and then hesitated. "Have you seen Kevin today? He left a note that he was going off with friends, but I expected him home by now."

Rachel shook her head. "No, Mum."

"Is Sarah here?"

Rachel stared up at her mistress. "No, Mum."

Maureen stared back and waited. "Are Sarah and Kevin off together?" Her tone was accusatory, almost cold.

A tear crept down Rachel's cheek. She withdrew a piece of paper from her apron pocket and held it out for Maureen who hesitated before taking the letter. She unfolded it and began to read.

Her face registered panic which became horror. "Gerald!

Gerald, come in here right now!"

Rachel burst into tears, burrowing her face in her hands. Maureen crossed around the island and placed a hand on her shoulder as Gerald entered from the dining room.

"What's wrong?" He stared at the two women. "What's going on?"

Maureen motioned to the letter lying on the counter top. "See for yourself."

Gerald picked up the letter and scanned its contents. His expression was at first one of surprise, but it soon settled into hardened determination. "What the hell?! Canada! Of course, Canada. Canada offers asylum to AIDS patients and their families." He dropped the letter and looked at Rachel.

"Did you know about this?"

She managed a muffled "No, sir," and sobbed.

"When did they leave?"

"I don't know. I woke at seven and found the letter lying on the counter."

Gerald looked at his watch. "Seven. We may still have time."

Maureen looked confused. "Time for what?"

"To catch them at the border." Gerald turned to leave. "I'm going to make some calls."

"No!" Maureen's voice was cold and firm. "If you stop them at the border, Sarah will be sent to Syracuse, and Kevin will be incarcerated!"

"I can't do anything to help Sarah, but I can certainly help my son!"

"No, Gerald! Your time to act has come and gone. Let them go. Maybe they can, at least, find some measure of happiness together."

Rachel began crying again.

Maureen wrapped her arms around her. "It's all right, dear. We'll get them back. Just not right now. But the day will come."

"I'm sorry, Mum . . . so, so sorry."

"Nonsense. We're all in this together." She stared up at Gerald. It was a look that would have turned most men to stone.

HALCYON'S DAYS

AUTHOR'S NOTE

Perhaps what follows isn't actually related to equinox at all. In a sense it is, but in a greater sense, it isn't. Those of you who are familiar with the *Star Trek* mythos should understand that the equinox theme was my own personal Kobayashi Maru. I spent a considerable amount of mental energy trying to devise a story around this anthology's theme without success.

Realizing that writing about the equinox was, for me, a no-win situation, I elected to change the rules ala James Tiberius Kirk and redefine equinox to suit my needs. One might argue that there is a touch of equinox, in the traditional sense, at work in this story. I'll acknowledge this much. But trust me, it was an afterthought. My interpretation in writing an equinox story was to reinvent equinox, or to at least contemplate it in a way that, I suspect, has never before been done. If nothing else, I think I've succeeded in this regard.

As for the actual writing of the tale, I began at the beginning, having little if any idea in which direction it would go. Like many stories, "Halcyon's Days" quickly assumed a life and direction of its own. From that point forward, I simply had to sit at the keyboard and fill in the details.

DY

HALCYON'S DAYS

David Yurkovich

1

HALCYON BLUNDELL STARED FORLORNLY at her desk as she switched off her laptop. Never before had the desk been so vacant, devoid as it was of paper, notepads, pens, and other office paraphernalia, all of which had been tossed absentmindedly into a cardboard box.

It was a busy Monday at 123 Pelham Street. The office, a hub of activity, but for all the wrong reasons. A soft, pasty man, early twenties with abstract eyebrows and dressed in a gray jumpsuit, hopped from workstation to workstation collecting laptops which he carried to a nearby office. A cordless drill was hastily removed from a black utility bag and the pasty man mechanically punched holes through the drive platters of each device.

Throughout the office, Halcyon's coworkers inattentively filled their own packing boxes. The usual activity of the office—constantly ringing phones, individuals dashing about madly to complete hurry-up-and-do-it-now requests from the field, daily status meetings, weapons requisitions, decryption of intercepted terrorist communiques—had been replaced by the sound of collapsed cardboard storage boxes being folded into shape before being hastily taped together. Family photos, coffee mugs, calendars, books—anything that wasn't deemed confidential or classified—were absently tossed in, one

149

item atop another atop another until the box was filled, at which point another box was erected.

No one spoke. There was nothing to say on this February morning, and nothing that might be said could change the reality faced by Halcyon and her coworkers. Whether they accepted it or not–and most didn't–there could be no doubt that EQUINOX was closing its doors forever.

The announcement had come suddenly, and most agreed that it had been unexpected, largely because the twelve field agents that comprised EQUINOX were the best in the world. Collectively, they'd previously served in MI5, the National Reconnaissance Office, the Office of Naval Intelligence, the General Directorate for Internal Security, and numerous other intelligence agencies globally. For the past six months, the majority of the team had been involved in unseating a South American drug and weapons manufacturing cartel known as El Hombre. The EQUINOX field team was days away from raiding El Hombre's headquarters when the order was given to stop all operations. Each EQUINOX agent was quickly reassigned to another high-profile intelligence community–they were too dangerous to allow the pursuit of freelance opportunities.

Halcyon and the office support staff were less fortunate–pink slips and a modest severance package along with an email message from the Assistant to the Director of the British Defense Intelligence Agency that briefly stated, "Best of luck in your future endeavors."

There were debriefings to attend and secrecy disclaimers to sign. So many papers that Halcyon's hand was sore by the time she'd signed the last of them. But overall, the dismissal of the EQUINOX in-house team was as routine as any organizational downsizing.

By 11:30 AM it was all over. The documentation and one-on-one meetings were complete and Halcyon, like her colleagues, was given a bulky envelope filled with helpful brochures specific to unemployment benefits, healthcare opportunities, counseling services. She tossed the envelope into the box she'd been packing and taped down the lid.

As she exited the office for the last time, Halcyon met with one final security officer who politely asked for her employee ID card and key FOB. The badge on his jacket read CARTER in red onyx uppercase letters. He was tall and lean with chocolate liquor skin, and Halcyon thought that if Carter were a tree, he might be a deciduous black

150

locust. She considered mentioning this to him as she surrendered the requested items, but declined as he sorted through the contents of her cardboard box.

"Can't leave with this, ma'am," he said, holding up a spiral-bound EQUINOX notebook.

"Are you kidding me? There's nothing in it. It's blank," Halcyon insisted, as Carter thumbed through it.

"Doesn't matter. Can't take it because of this." He pointed at the EQUINOX logo on the laminated cardstock cover.

"It's just a bloody insignia."

Without a moment's hesitation, Carter ripped the cover from the notebook and tossed it into a narrow trashcan marked HAZARD, before placing the remainder of the notebook back into the box.

"It's okay now." Carter secured the lid back onto the box and presented it to Halcyon. "Have a nice day," he offered.

"That's very kind of you," Halcyon said, "but I have other plans." She stepped out into the blustery February air and stared across the street at Russell Square where she'd so often lunched, wondering if she'd ever have occasion to visit the park again. It was doubtful. Halcyon headed north, arriving at the Euston Square Station within a few minutes.

The London Overground was standing-room only. As she stood on the bus, right hand listlessly holding onto an overhead support strap, Halcyon thought about how strangely quiet her departure had been. She was struck by the sudden realization that in her fifteen years with EQUINOX, she'd never lunched with a coworker, attended an after-work happy hour, or gotten to know any of the personal details of Phyllis Dreadmoor, Pete Maars, Gabriella Gomez, or any of the others with whom she'd shared office space. While it was true that EQUINOX frowned upon team member socialization, many of the office staff were, in fact, friends outside the office. Halcyon wanted none of it. In her world, work was work and home was home. There was no mixing of the two. By the time the bus arrived at her stop, Halcyon wondered why she'd never allowed the two to meet, even sporadically. She realized it was too late for regrets and upon further reflection felt pleased that across her many years of employment with EQUINOX she'd never compromised her principles.

Far more than the employees, what Halcyon was going to miss—was already missing—was the work. A living lifeline to a complete stranger. It had been her role at EQUINOX and she'd excelled in it. It seemed like someone was always in trouble. She'd lost count of the number of times O'Brien had phoned and requested an underground path to guide him through one remote city after the other. Or the requisitions for special clearance that enabled Clarkson to infiltrate the Cuban drug empire overseen by the Hernandez brothers.

Eighteen minutes later she arrived at Stonebridge Park. She strode north along Tokyngton Avenue and passed an elderly woman. The pinback button on her teal raincoat read WHEN ONE DOOR CLOSES, ANOTHER OPENS.

"How soon before that happens?" Halcyon asked, pointing at the button.

"It varies. In your case, I'd say a while."

"I haven't got a while."

The woman adjusted her broom bristle hair as an angry wind tossed it about. "In that case, wait until April."

"Why April?"

"Why not April?"

Halcyon watched as the older woman continued south, favoring her right leg with each step. She hailed a taxi and glanced back at Halcyon. "Big changes are in store. April 7, if I had to wager a guess. Wait for it." The back door to the taxi swung shut and sped away.

"Tosspot," Halcyon whispered. She soon reached home, undid a dozen door locks, and stepped inside, closing the door behind her. "One door closes, another opens," she said doubtfully, as Cat, her sole pet for the past eight years, meowed hello. Halcyon hung her coat and scarf then extended a hand downward and stroked the brown and white fur of the creature's chin. Cat purred approvingly before turning his attention to a chaffinch perched on the flower box outside the kitchen window.

Halcyon glanced at her left hand and the rubber bands around three of her fingers. Long ago, she'd developed a reminder system involving rubber bands. Each represented unfinished business.

Red band, middle finger: Staff dossier reviews

Blue band, index finger: Monthly munitions order

Yellow band, ring finger: Transcribe minutes from weekly debriefing sessions

"Won't be needing you anymore." She casually removed the objects and tossed them onto a nearby coffee table. She thought about switching on the laptop, updating her resume, and beginning the horrid process of seeking employment at fifty-four years of age, but realized she lacked the mental energy for more than TV. The job search could wait.

After boiling water for tea, Halcyon slipped into comfortable sweats and a t-shirt before settling in front of the telly. She toggled past BBC One and BBC Two before stopping at ITV London and the early news. Halcyon wasn't surprised to find no coverage about the closing of EQUINOX. Unlike MI5, NCA, DI, JIO, and other British intelligence agencies that were known to the public, EQUINOX had maintained a level of stealth unsurpassed in contemporary society, though she knew the company's history well. Formed in 1939 at a time when MI5 was faltering, EQUINOX initially consisted of five operatives. This number swelled to twelve during the height of World War II and had remained unchanged in successive decades. The team was supported by ten office staffers. The Home Secretary believed that a smaller organization stood a greater chance of remaining clandestine. The theory proved accurate, as secrets remained secret, decade upon decade, and EQUINOX remained unknown to all but the highest-ranking members of Parliament. And with the agency's demise—its computers wiped or destroyed, its files incinerated, its field agents reassigned—there was simply no chance the existence of England's Quintessential Undercover Intelligence Network – OXford, would ever come to light.

Halcyon pondered this and suddenly realized that there were, in fact, ten chances, of which she was one.

2

The days passed slowly as Halcyon began the task of finding new work. Her resume contained no mention of EQUINOX, but instead was filled with employers she'd never known and positions she'd never held, all of which she realized would be validated through the intelligence network's clandestine Office of Faux Employment History. She registered with Universal Jobmatch, Reed, NHS Jobs, and a few other sites, but did little actual searching.

Sleep was difficult. She frequently remained indoors. On days when she ventured out, Halcyon grew increasingly paranoid that she was being followed. But as February bled into March, Halcyon's paranoia eased. She reasoned that if the British Government had wanted to silence her, they'd had ample opportunity. Nonetheless, the curtains in her flat remained drawn day and night.

In her work with EQUINOX she'd often provided support when it came to tying up loose ends. It was known as white boarding. Sometimes white boarding occurred within hours, sometimes days. Sometimes years. However long it took to erase the white board. The curtains remained drawn into April.

Halcyon increasingly watched television and spent less time reading. No news. News was reality and she was avoiding reality, as evidenced by the two dozen untouched *Daily Telegraphs* stacked on a living room end table.

Her mobile rang on the morning of April 5, the caller ID read as UNKNOWN. A potential employer, though most likely a robocaller.

"Hello?" she asked, to no reply. "Is someone there?"

A friendly male voice answered her question with a question. "Who's this?"

"I know who I am," Halcyon said. "Who might you be?"

"I might be any number of people, mightn't I? I might be Charles Darwin, or perhaps Jack the Ripper. That's not important. What's important is that I know who you are. I know all about you, Halcyon Blundell."

She fell silent, mind racing to identify the voice. "What do you want?" she asked, stalling for more time and information.

"We should talk. Perhaps I could drop by for tea and biscuits. You've been at 424 Luddington for seven year. I'm assuming you're still there?"

She paused, calling forth skills nearly forgotten from a prior training session in dialect recognition. Male caller. Gruff voice. Smoker. Knows where I live. Diphthongal pronunciation of *four*, indicating an older speaker. Knows. Where. I. Live. Absence of a plural marker in *year*. Both traits indicative of the Yorkshire area.

"Why would I meet with you? I don't even know you."

"Let me refresh your memory." The stranger paused for a moment then spoke with a quiet intensity. *"This is Melville, requesting Intel on Candice's Peacock."*

It was Halcyon's turn to pause. "Melville? You don't . . . sound like Melville."

"Of course I don't. For once I'm not speaking through a voice modulator."

"What do you want?"

"We need to talk."

"We are talking."

"In person."

"Why?"

"You really don't know?"

"Enlighten me," Halcyon insisted.

"You subscribe to *The Telegraph*."

She considered asking how Melville knew this, but realized that, assuming it *was* Melville, her life was no longer private.

"Look at yesterday's edition. Page two, first column. I'll wait."

Halcyon retrieved the newspaper as instructed.

"Bleetham Tower Suicide. Phyllis Dreadmoor?"

"Seems your ex-colleague took a swan dive from the forty-seventh floor, which is most peculiar given that the top five floors of the building are restricted without the proper credentials–credentials she didn't have."

"So . . . probably not a suicide."

"Anything's possible. Phyllis was a happy woman with everything ahead of her. Following EQUINOX she'd already found employment with the Ministry of Agriculture. Aside from that, she was acrophobic and would have sooner gouged her eyes out than gone to the top of a high rise. You might also want to Google search Pete Maars, your former colleague from Encryption and Decryption."

"Deceased?"

"March 17. Accidental drowning in five feet of water."

"It happens."

"As I said before, anything's possible. Did you know that before joining EQUINOX, Pete worked as a swimming instructor?"

"Jesus Christ." Halcyon paused, then asked the question, regretting the words before they were fully formed. "Are you . . . coming to kill me?"

Melville chuckled. "You've worked with me for nearly ten years.

Surely you must know I'm more original than that."

"Yes. I suppose you are."

"There's a coffee shop you typically visit on alternate Wednesday evenings. McCaffery's Brew on Parchment Street."

"I suppose you also know my drink of choice."

"Earl Grey, though you occasional dabble with espresso."

"Occasionally."

"Meet me there tomorrow night, seven o'clock."

"How will I recognize you?"

"I'll be the one in the black trench with matching fedora. I'm kidding. But don't worry, I'll recognize you. See you then."

"Can't hardly wait."

"And Halcyon, about your closed curtains . . ."

"Yes."

"Keep them closed."

3

Halcyon endured a restless night as questions with no answers raced through her head. Was she in danger? Why had Melville contacted her and why did he want to meet with her in person? Who killed Phyllis Dreadmoor and Pete Maars? Were her other ex-coworkers still alive, or had their deaths simply not made the papers? How could she protect herself?

Sleep finally arrived just before sunup and Halcyon dozed until early afternoon. She awoke feeling relieved as two o'clock approached. Less time to kill until 7:00 PM, she thought, and her arms erupted with a wave of goosebumps at the peculiarity of the phrase itself. Was it time to kill? Or, more precisely, to be killed?

The afternoon crawled slowly by and Halcyon spent the hours sorting through the many newspapers that had accumulated in her flat, fearful that news of another ex-colleague's demise may lie within the black and white pages. She felt some relief when the search yielded no results.

Five o'clock arrived and she showered and dressed, determined to show up well in advance of the scheduled meeting time with Melville. She opted for fleece lightweight jogging pants, a long-sleeve tee, track jacket, and sneakers, her mind conjuring up scenarios in which she'd need to flee for her life. She threw her mobile and a small kitchen knife into a cross-body handbag and headed out the front door while Cat slept on the living room rug.

A light rain fell as she reached McCaffery's. Its familiar jazz feed felt especially appropriate for the weather. The shop was empty but for three customers. A teenage couple sat near the entrance, hands locked together with youthful passion as their beverages grew cold. Near the back of the shop an elderly man sat on a weathered sofa discretely ogling two women in short skirts who stood outside and hailed a taxi. Halcyon ordered Earl Grey and found a seat against the wall that gave her a view of the entire shop. No one could enter or leave without her noticing. She retrieved her mobile. It was 5:30.

By 7:30 PM, the light rain had evolved into a heavy downpour. Halcyon thought that might account for Melville's absence, but she tired of waiting. The distance home was short, and although she had no umbrella, she realized that she could run it in under five minutes. As she stood up, a fortyish man suddenly entered, breathless.

"Bloody useless," he said, a torn umbrella in his right hand. He approached the counter and wiped the rain from his face with a paper napkin.

"Flat white," he said to the barista, as rainwater dripped from his hair and onto the counter. He called over to Halcyon. "Earl Grey was it?"

Halcyon nodded and sat back down.

"Bit more volume, guv," Melville said, pointing at the overhead speakers and placing a tenner into the tip jar. "Huge fan."

Shortly thereafter, as Miles Davis's "Kind of Blue" reverberated throughout the shop, Melville approached Halcyon's table with drinks in hand. He placed a saturated jacket over the back of a chair and sat down across from her.

"It's funny," she said, "you work with someone but never see them, and you form an image of what they look like, and then, when you meet them, it turns out you were completely off."

"How so?"

"I'd always pictured you to be a large bloke, fifteen stone, deep-recessed eyes, square jaw, butcher hands, and a cunning moustache, but you're nothing of the sort."

"Butcher hands? I'll try to take that as a complement. You look exactly like your photo."

"I don't know whether to feel flattered or creeped out."

"It's my job to know about people."

"I suppose so. I have to say, Agent Melville . . ."

"Just Melville."

"I have to say, Just Melville, that I was expecting something more akin to an intelligence community cloak and dagger act from you," Halcyon said.

"How so?"

"You're entrance, for example. Wasn't exactly stealth."

"On the contrary, Ms. Blundell. Sometimes the most indiscrete entrance is the one that lacks any and all discretion. I've learned that over the years."

"Yes. I'm sure you have. So why did you wish to see me? Am I in danger?"

"There are always a few, trigger-happy rogue agents within any organization. Paranoia runs deep with my kind. But I think at this point you needn't be worried over that."

"Trigger-happy?"

"Here's the thing of it," Melville said. He spoke softly but not in a whisper. "Not long ago, loyalty meant something. Yet, somewhere along the way, that value was assigned a pound note and things haven't been the same since."

"You talk as if betrayal were something new, Just Melville. It's as old as Judas Iscariot and Ephialtes, and let's not forget our own Benedict Arnold and Guy Fawkes."

"A valid point, Ms. Blundell. I'm only mentioning this to help you understand why Pete Maars and Phyllis Dreadmoor were silenced. EQUINOX, as you're well aware, has come and gone, and it came and went without a single member of the public knowing about the great and terrible operations it conducted. There's enough distrust for the government as it is. Can't have ex-staffers like Pete or Phyllis telling company secrets to hungry tabloid journalists at *The Sun* or *The Daily Mail*. That simply won't do."

"Are you serious?"

"Quite."

"Did you personally . . . were you the one who . . ."

"That isn't what I do," Melville said. "I'll give this to you straight. When the Assistant Deputy disbanded EQUINOX, he fucked everything up. Sadly, he's still employed, but has been kicked down the ladder significantly. Fact is, the entirety of EQUINOX was supposed to be reassigned, not merely the field agents. Little wonder Maars and Dreadmoor were planning to violate the termination agreements they signed in February when the doors closed. They were screwed over. You all were. And now the PM is scared shitless, afraid that you or one of the other team mates will tell tales out of school. You with me so far?"

Halcyon nodded.

"Good. Here's the thing: No one wants more spilled blood. The government owes everyone who worked for EQUINOX a debt of gratitude. To that end, you're going to receive a generous offer. I'm merely a messenger."

"First of all, I wouldn't talk, because I *do* know what loyalty means. Secondly, even if I take this mysterious offer, how do you or the PM or the Queen herself know that one day I won't sell out? Where's your guarantee? And for that matter, where's mine? How do I wake up every morning confident that I'm not going to be pushed in front of an oncoming train or strangled with piano wire? How do I know there's not a white board with my name on it?"

"The guarantee is at 12500 Coventry."

Halcyon paused. This wasn't the answer she'd been expecting.

"What the hell's at 12500 Coventry?"

"As I said . . . the guarantee."

4

Melville's exit from the coffee shop held far less fanfare than his arrival. Before departing, he quietly slid a #10 self-seal white business envelope across to Halcyon.

"What's this?"

"Tomorrow morning at 10:00 AM you will visit 12500 Coventry. You will present this envelope to the front desk staff. You will not be asked to provide identification as they are expecting you."

"Sounds scrummy," she said in her best Mary Berry. "Any insights you'd like to share?"

"None."

"I have a cat. His name's Cat."

"That's certainly an easy name to remember."

"Promise me that if anything . . . bad happens, you'll see that he's looked after."

"I promise. But nothing bad is going to happen to you. You'll be fine."

Melville stood, and with a nod and a smile left the building.

Halcyon hung around the shop for several minutes. She felt both relief and paranoia. Upon placing the envelope into an interior jacket pocket she started for home, her swift walk erupting into a feverish run atop the rain-soaked sidewalks.

Minutes later, from the presumed safety and privacy of her flat, Halcyon tore open the envelope and unfolded a single sheet of photocopy paper which consisted of three short lines of uppercase text.

HALCYON BLUNDELL
NINO QQ123456C
ME1+PI

The document included a stamped seal of the Office of the Prime Minister as well as her signature. Halcyon folded the paper and placed it back into the envelope.

For the next several hours she sought to learn everything possible about 12500 Coventry courtesy of Google, but aside from discovering that it was adjacent to a multiplex and a fitness center, her search bore no fruit.

Halcyon learned even less about the alphanumeric sequence ME1+PI. Frustrated, she sought comfort in hot tea and a fresh pack of Happy Faces biscuits while channel surfing.

Near midnight she drew a warm bath and dozed briefly within the soothing water.

Before departing for her morning appointment, Halcyon put down extra food and water for Cat, who purred in blissful ignorance. Partially because she trusted Melville and partially because she felt as if she had no choice *but* to trust him, Halcyon was soon aboard the West Midland train en route to Camden Town.

Forty-five minutes later, she arrived at her destination—a postmodern, four-story edifice of bronze pillars and mushroom glass. She walked through an automated revolving door and continued across the lobby, her loafers echoing upon the polished tile floor.

Halcyon approached the front desk and presented the envelope to an elderly male dressed in a gray double-breasted jacket with an enamel pin bearing the Royal Coat of Arms of the United Kingdom on his lapel.

"Nice pin," she said.

He smiled at Halcyon with blisteringly white teeth. "This envelope has been opened."

"I was curious," she said, nonplused.

"Everything seems to be in order, Ms. Blundell. National Insurance Number: QQ123456C." He paused. "ME1+PI. Interesting."

"Yeah, I'm not sure what that's about."

The whitest whites she'd ever seen grimaced as Halcyon was handed a hardbound ledger and fountain pen. "Sign and date here, please."

"I just realized, today's the seventh of April."

"Indeed. What about it?"

"It's probably nothing. Not too long ago, I was told to expect big changes on this day."

"I'd say you've come to the right place." The smile faded from the old man's face. "Fourth floor. Elevators are on the right."

It was a long conversation. The room was sterile but warm. She sat and sipped water as she was shown statistics, charts, outlines, and summaries of published studies. She was assured that, from a patient safety perspective, it was all well and good. She was told it was the only way. She continued to sip the water. She understood the logic, and it sounded safe enough. But by the end of the discussion she wanted to run. Her mind pleaded with her body. *Get out of here. Flee.* She tried to stand but couldn't. She glanced down, expecting to find her legs shackled. There were no chains. Her body simply wouldn't cooperate. She stared at glass of water—nearly empty, she'd drunk so much and hadn't it tasted somewhat off? She tried, without success, to wiggle her toes and move her feet. She tried to panic but her mind seemed incapable. She exhaled slowly.

They promised she'd be safe. And more than anything she wanted to be safe. A pen found its way onto her hand and her hand found its way onto a crowded legal document. She scratched a line across the bottom of a form, fingers barely able to grasp the instrument, and was helped to her feet and onto a gurney that she was certain hadn't been there earlier.

The lights overhead were bright but soft, like miniature suns behind thin clouds. She counted the lights as the gurney rolled from room to room, finally stopping in a large chamber with high ceilings and ducts that blew cold air. She felt the tightness in her right forearm as the tourniquet was tied, the cool dampness of the disinfectant upon her skin, the pinch of a needle being pressed into her vein. Soon she felt no anxiety, no fear as unconsciousness arrived seconds later.

Halcyon awoke in her flat on a Sunday morning. She felt tired and couldn't quite remember where she'd been the night before. She picked up an empty wine bottle from the coffee table, and although she had no recollection of having drunk wine, she reasoned that the wine was likely the reason she lacked recollection. She spent much of the day on the sofa and channel surfed, her mind a fog like that which hung over the city.

She returned to work the following day. Just another rainy Monday with the insurance firm of Riddle and Riddle. As she often did, Halcyon lunched with Sally Kirkland, the firm's top regional sales manager. The pair had joined the firm on the same day, nearly one year ago, and had become fast friends.

Monday afternoon passed quickly and soon the first day of the work week was history.

"Off to the pub?" Sally asked, as Halcyon packed up her attache.

"Wouldn't be a Monday without a stop at Ricky's. Coming?"

"Too many contracts to review. Have a pint for me."

The rain continued throughout most of the week but ended late Friday afternoon just in time for the weekend. Sally and Halcyon headed out to happy hour to get an early jump on it.

"Almost forgot my book," Sally said, as the two women headed toward the elevator banks. She ran back and tucked the well-worn paperback into her handbag.

"What are you reading now?"

"The latest Olivia Bannister thriller. This one's about a woman working for a super-secret spy organization. Life is grand until one day the agency is abruptly shut down by the powers that be, and she loses her job. Thing is, she's got a lot of important information inside her noodle."

"Wouldn't the easy thing be to simply kill her off? Keep the secrets secret?" Halcyon asked, pressing the elevator's down button.

"You'd think so. But I guess out of a sense of loyalty, or perhaps because they needed a good test case, she's sent to a medical facility for a procedure known as medical erasure and insertion."

"What's that?"

The women stepped into the lift. "Take out the top-secret memories and replace them with drivel. She calls it ME1+PI. I call it bollocks."

"Seems plausible."

"It isn't. There's also tons of exposition. Technical terms like *synaptic strength* and *long-term potentiation*. Rather distances the reader." Sally stared at Halcyon who was applying fresh lipstick.

"So what happens?"

"The operation succeeds. Years of memories are selectively wiped out and replaced with new ones. She's placed into a new job. There's a puffed-up subplot where one of the memory implants involves a best friend, though of course it's *not* a best friend at all like you and me, but a field operative whose job is to make sure that little miss can't remember shit, still can't remember shit."

"How's it end?"

"Haven't gotten there yet, but I think it's going to work out okay for her. You can borrow it when I'm done."

Halcyon laughed as the elevator doors opened. "Thanks, but I think I'll wait for the movie."

Upon arriving at the pub, Halcyon made a detour to the ladies room. Sally used the time to compose a text message, consisting of two lines, to an unpublished number:

1-WK REVIEW COMPLETE.
ALL CLEAR.

Over drinks, Sally broke the news to Halcyon.

"Why didn't you tell me sooner?"

"Couldn't. You know how these things are. Only got the news today."

"I'm happy for you, of course, but Madrid? Starting Monday? I'll never see you."

"Of course you will. I'm sure I'll have occasion to check up on you from time to time." Sally forced a smile, aware of the carelessness of her words, and quickly moved along. "Anyway, promotions like this are few and far between. I just couldn't say no."

"I'll miss you. I don't even know what else to say."

"Say congratulations, silly. And buy the next round."

The weeks that followed became months, and before long the year reached an end. Halcyon's days were, in fact, halcyon days. She woke each morning feeling unusually happy and peaceful, content in her work and in her life.

The New Year passed quickly and spring approached. She overslept on March 20 and missed the early bus. As rain poured from the sky, Halcyon stood beneath an umbrella awaiting the arrival of the 10:15. An elderly woman with thin spaghetti hair and dressed in a teal raincoat limped toward her.

"Bloody rain. Can't even sit down."

Halcyon smiled politely. "Have we met before?"

"Maybe we have. Maybe we haven't. I meet a lot of people."

"This weather. Wouldn't even know it's the equinox."

"Sorry?"

"Twice a year the day and night are the same length. Didn't you attend a proper school as a child?" Halcyon seemed adrift. "I swear the education system in this country has been in the gutter since the formation of the NHS in '48."

Halcyon turned away from the woman and stared into the distance. "Equinox," she said softly.

AUTHOR BIOS

BEALS

DD Beals was born in Brooklyn, New York. The daughter of an NYC taxi driver, she learned early that people can share intimate details of their lives in just ten minutes Hearing her father's stories started her interest in writing. Ms. Beals has worked for local, state, and the federal government, writing policy and developing new programs. She currently splits her time between Maryland and Delaware and is a member of the Milton Workshop and the Rehoboth Beach Writers Guild. Along with her dog, Sam, she enjoys a rainy day, good coffee, and a view of nature.

CRANDELL

William F. Crandell returned home from the Vietnam War with a taste for adventure, a skeptic's eye, and a hundred thousand stories. Completing a doctorate in history at Ohio State University, he was awarded a Maryland State Arts Council Individual Artist Award in 2004 for his mystery novel, *Let's Say Jack Kennedy Killed the Girl*. Bill has published numerous short stories, book reviews, and political analyses. He was awarded the PRIZM's Mark Twain Award for Humor/Social Commentary 2012 and resides in Milton with his wife, Judith.

DUTTON

David W. Dutton is a semi-retired residential designer who was born and raised in Milton, DE. He has written two novels, several short stories, and eleven plays. His musical comedy, *oh! Maggie*, in collaboration with Martin Dusbiber, was produced by the Possum Point Players and the Lake Forest Drama Club. He wrote two musical reviews for the Possum Point Players: *An Evening With Cole Porter*, in collaboration with Marcia Faulkner, and *With a Song in My Heart*. He also wrote the one-act play, *Why the Chicken Crossed the Road*, commissioned and produced by the Delmarva Chicken Festival. In 1997, he was awarded a fellowship as an established writer by the Delaware Arts Council. In 1998, he received a first-place award for his creative nonfiction by the Delaware Literary Connection. His piece, "Who is Nahnu Dugeye?" was subsequently published in the literary anthology, *Terrains*. In conjunction with the Milton Workshop, he is completing his third novel, *One of the Madding Crowd*. David, his wife, Marilyn, and their Rottweiler, Molly, currently reside in Milton.

LEWES
TJ Lewes hails from Cherry Valley, Pennsylvania, with degrees from Lebanon Valley College, El Colegio de España, and Delaware State University in Spanish, Philosophy of Religion, and Education. Before writing, Lewes pursued a seventeen-year teaching career in High School, College, and Medical Spanish, English Literature and Effective Communications, English as a Second Language, Aquatic Fitness, and Immigrant Citizenship. She was honored in Who's Who Among America's Teachers, Biltmore's Who's Who, and Covington's Who's Who. An adventurer at heart, Lewes has traveled extensively through Central and South America studying pre-Colombian civilizations. She has taught and traveled in China, is certified under the AFF in skydiving, is resort-certified in Scuba, and is now embracing her biggest adventure: raising her two children in Sussex County. Lewes is currently completing two novels. Her recent publications include the short stories, "El Día de Los Angelitos Inocentes" and "The Snow Monkey."

NORTHERN
After publishing the Executive Summary to "The Future of Independent Life Insurance Distribution," Bayne Northern transitioned from writing nonfiction to fiction. She is currently completing her first novel, *The Bitch Seat*, situated in the financial services industry. An avid short story author, Bayne is also an active volunteer of the Village Improvement Association, a resident of Rehoboth Beach, and a proud owner of Thatcher, the corgi.

PEARCE
Dianne Pearce founded The Milton Workshop in 2015. She is a graduate of both the West Chester University and Vermont College writing programs, earning an MA and an MFA. Dianne has taught

writing in Delaware, California, Pennsylvania, and Maryland. She sometimes takes on editing projects for other writers, and has done both writing and advocacy for causes close to her heart, among them adoption, developmental disabilities, and animals. Dianne loves living in Milton, and claims to have read *Paradise Lost* in her youth, the real version where all the S-es look like Fs, which she says must count for something.

POLO

Mark Alan Polo has been an interior designer for over thirty years and is President and Owner of The Urban Dweller/Polo M.A. Inc., with offices in Northern New Jersey and a satellite office in Delaware. Mark became a permanent Delaware resident in 2014. A part-time writer for the past fifteen years, Mark's recent short story, "Fifty-Five," appeared in the 2016 award-winning *Beach Nights* anthology (Cat and Mouse Press). His debut novel, *Mosquitoes and Men*, is slated for publication in 2018. He is at work on a second novel.

SPEIZER CRANDELL

Judith Speizer Crandell is an award-winning writer and teacher of fiction, poetry, and nonfiction. She's received residencies at Yaddo, AROHO (A Room of One's Own), and a Maryland State Arts Council Individual Artist Fellowship for her novel, *The Resurrection of Hundreds Feldman*. She has performed readings at the New York State Writers Institute, the New York State Vietnam Veterans Memorial, and the Washington, DC, and Cleveland Public Libraries. A journalist and Washington, DC, speechwriter for nearly twenty years, she moved to Milton, DE, in July to be near the ocean and write.

SZ KEANE

Carrie Sz Keane studied journalism and English at the University of Maryland and later apprenticed as a midwife in rural Kentucky before studying nurse-midwifery at Yale University. While at Yale, Keane was awarded a humanities honor in creative writing with her piece entitled "Modern Nurse Nancy," a story about working a night shift as a new nurse on a postpartum unit, which was later published in a Canadian nursing textbook. Upon graduating in 2004, Keane has been journaling and writing the stories of her work as a midwife and her relationship with her patients and the community of Sussex

County Delaware. She is actively writing a journalistic memoir of her career. Ms. Keane works at Planned Parenthood of Delaware as a sexual health clinician providing contraception, annual examinations, STD screenings, and treatment for males and females.

YURKOVICH

Milton-based author David is a former (2017) Delaware Division of the Arts literature fellow. David began writing in 1992 with a focus on graphic novels and comics. His first self-published comic was funded by a grant by the Xeric Foundation in 1994. As a writer and illustrator, his works include *Death by Chocolate* and *Less Than Heroes* (both published by Top Shelf Productions) and *Altercations* (published by Sleeping Giant). In 2007 David wrote, designed, and published *Mantlo: A Life in Comics*, a benefit magazine to help aid in the medical expenses of Bill Mantlo (creator of Rocket Raccoon, Cloak and Dagger, and other Marvel properties). In 2016, David was selected to attend the Delaware Seashore Poetry & Prose Writers' Retreat. In addition to short stories and essays (with publishers including Marvel), he has published two prose novels, *Glass Onion* and *Banana Seat Summer*, and is completing two manuscripts. Most recently, David penned an essay for an upcoming book about the English rock band XTC. David frequently posts new serialized fiction and sequential art at: davidyurkovich.wordpress.com.

Made in the USA
Columbia, SC
29 May 2018